Lighthouses of the Golden State

California's Shining Beacons

Lighthouses of the Golden State

California's Shining Beacons

By Kent Barclay Weymouth

Magpie Publishing Inc.
Sacramento, California

To order additional copies, please contact us.

contact@calights.net

Library of Congress Catalog Card Number: 2008901062

ISBN 978-0-9798913-0-4

For original artwork of California's majestic lighthouses
by Kent Weymouth

Visit

www.TheCanvasDigital.com

For more information on California Lighthouses
Visit

www.Calights.net

Cover photos and book design by Kent Weymouth

Printed in the United States of America

FOR JANE AND GEORGE

"Oh, what is the bane of a light-keeper's life?

That causes him worry, struggles, and strife,

That makes him use cuss words and beat up his wife,

It's Brass work.

What makes him look ghastly, consumptive, and thin?

What robs him of health and vigor and vim?

And causes despair and drives him to sin?

It's Brass work.

The Devil himself could not ever invent

A material causing more worldwide lament

And Uncle Sam's service 'bout ninety percent

It's Brass work.

The lamp in the tower, reflector, and shade,

The tools and accessories pass in parade

As a matter of fact the whole outfit is made

Of Brass work.

The machinery, clockwork and fog signal bell,

The coal-hoods, the dustpans, the pump in the well,

Now I'll leave it to you mates, if this isn't---well

Brass work.

I dug, scrub and polish, and work with a might,

And just when I get it all shiny and bright,

In comes the fog like a thief in the night,

Goodbye Brass work.

Oh, why should the spirit of mortal be proud?

In this short span of life that he is allowed

If all of the lining in every darn cloud

Is Brass work?

And when I have polished until I am cold,

And I'm taken aloft to the Heavenly fold,

Will my harp and my crown be made of pure gold?

No, Brass work."

Fred Morong, Light-keeper of the Point Reyes Light Station

TABLE OF CONTENTS

Acknowledgements 1

Introduction 3

Lighting the Gold Coast! 6

Lighthouse Administrations 7

Light-keepers 9

The Lens 11

Style 14

Lighting the South 17

Old Point Loma 19

New Point Loma 22

Ballast Point 24

Long Beach Robot Light 26

L. A. Harbor (Angels Gate) 27

Point Fermin 31

Point Vicente 36

Point Hueneme 38

Anacapa Island 41

Santa Barbara Lighthouse 44

Point Conception 46

Point Arguello 50

San Luis Obispo 53

Piedras Blancas 55

Point Sur 58

Point Pinos 61

Santa Cruz Lighthouse 66

Año Nuevo Island 70

Pigeon Point Light Station 74

Point Montara 77

Rubicon Point 79

San Francisco Bay Lights 81

Roe Island 83

Carquinez Strait 86

Mare Island 88

Oakland Harbor 90

East Brother Island 93

Southampton Shoals 98

Yerba Buena 102

Alcatraz Island Lighthouse 104

Angel Island State Park 108

Fort Point 111

Lime Point 114

Mile Rock 117

Point Bonita 122

Farallon Island 125

Lighting the North 137

Point Reyes 139

Point Arena 146

Point Cabrillo 156

Punta Gorda 161

Lightship WLV 605 163

Cape Mendocino 166

Table Bluff Lighthouse 170

Humboldt Harbour Light 172

Trinidad Head Lighthouse 174

Battery Point 177

St. George Reef 184

Bibliography 194

Index 197

Recommended Websites 200

Acknowledgements

First, a very special thanks to Jane and George Wooden, a constant inspiration of patience and support without whose guidance, this book would not have been possible.

My deep appreciation to Jeff Gales, the executive director and Wayne Wheeler the president of the *United States Lighthouse Society* who provided access to many of the documents needed in assembling this book.

The United States Coast Guard has been exceptionally courteous in providing my assistants and me the time and admittance to those lighthouses not accessible to the public. Those men of the Coast Guard's "Aids to Navigation Teams" went out of their way, and I am eternally grateful for the help they provided. The following individuals were particularly helpful: Chief Chris Nylan, and EM3 Javier Lopez from the San Diego team, BMC Chief David Bullard, and EM1 Chad Rous from the Los Angeles team, Kim Castrobran, the light-keeper of Point Hueneme and his father Eric Castrobran, the light-keeper of the Point Vicente Light Station, Robert Steiz, and Lt. Russell from the Santa Barbara team, BMC S. Elasser, and John "Mike" Hensley "Special Aid to Vice Admiral Johnson" in the Bay Area, Chief Petty Officer BM1 J. Zappen, Exec Petty Officer EM2 M. Payne, Chief Rob Shafer, and Chief Petty Officer Chris Jones from the Humboldt team.

My gratitude to those individuals who welcomed me into their respective lighthouses: John Bogacki, the BLM Site Manager of Piedras Blancas Light Station, San Luis Obispo Lighthouse docents Sally Krenn, and Dana Tryde as well as Kathy Gregory, and Kristen Childs from Point Fermin. Gary Strachen, State Park Ranger at Año Nuevo, Chris Bowman from the Point Montara Lighthouse, and Lucien and Isabella Spellman, light-keepers of the East Brother Lighthouse. For their kind help with access to Southampton Shoals Lighthouse, thanks to Marson O. Kay, the Manager of Tinsley Island, as well as David Nightingale and Terry Klaus the "Commodore" of the St. Francis Yacht Club. Thanks to Rae Radtkey at Point Arena, and Executive Director Jim Kimbrough, and Lisa Wigg from Point Cabrillo. Thank you to Rick Heiser and Guy Towers from the St. George Reef Lighthouse Preservation Society.

My appreciation goes to Brad and Bobi Lundberg, Resident Managers from the Bixby Ranch Corp. for their cooperation, and Stuart Titus from the Humboldt County Fairgrounds.

Thanks to the following historical societies and libraries that provided additional archive material helpful in the research for this book: Bob Munson, historian of the "Cabrillo National Monument," the "San Pedro Bay Historical Society," Charles Johnson, "Librarian and Archivist" for the Ventura County Museum of History and Art, the Santa Barbara History Museum, the San Luis Obispo County Library, and the San Luis Obispo County Museum, the Humboldt Historical Society, and Linda Ging and Sean Smith from the Del Norte Historical Society.

Many thanks to the following people: Douglas Peterson, Historical Archivist for the California Maritime Academy, Jim Kerner from the Vallejo Naval and Historical Museum, John Byrne, Executive Officer of the Lightship Relief WLV 605, and Jesus "Chuy" Rodriguez-Salinas a State Park Ranger from Angel Island who toured me around the island to visit all three historic sites.

I would also like to thank my two assistants, Darryl Rosingana, and Annette Daniel for all of their help while I photographed each of the lighthouses, and for keeping me company on the road as we traveled throughout the state. Thanks to Barbara Howrey for doing the copy edit of the book, and John Dorrance, my lifelong friend, for his expertise and guidance in crafting this book.

INTRODUCTION

The golden age of the lighthouse has passed by, but the edifices of many lighthouses remain throughout California, entering a new era in their long stormy lives. Technology has replaced the huge Fresnel lens with small efficient automated beacons. These beacons are quite capable of doing the job once held by hardy adventurous individuals, who spent lonely years tending the lights to stay ships on their course. Not all of these structures are still standing, and many are not accessible to the public.

From the beginning, it has been my desire to be as inclusive as I can in listing all of the lights of interest in California, so private aids to navigation, technically, not lighthouses, are included as well. If you are a traveler, lighthouse enthusiast, or lighthouse expert, I hope this book offers you a glimpse into California's lighthouses that you have not seen before. I have organized this book to unfold from south to north.

The great state of California over the years has had a total of 43 working light stations or lighthouses. Seven private aids to navigation constructed in a similar style to a lighthouse are found on our shore but have never housed a light-keeper. A replica of Cape Mendocino, located at the entrance to the Humboldt County fairgrounds, welcomes visitors year round. A replica of Trinidad Head, built as a memorial to the men of the community lost to the sea, stands proudly overlooking Trinidad Bay. Today California once again has 43 structures actually standing, between replicas, actual lighthouses and their cousins, the private aid. Of the original lighthouses, 30 stand as active aids to navigation. Most are well maintained and stay in a ready state of repair due to the diligence of the United States Coast Guard.

Six lighthouses are now part of our National Parks Service (Point Reyes, Point Bonita, Alcatraz Island, Fort Point, Anacapa Island, and Old Point Loma). Six lighthouses are designated as State Parks (Año Nuevo, Pigeon Point, Point Montara, and the three Angel Island lights), and one is a City Park (Point Fermin). Four lighthouses (Point Arena, Point Pinos, Battery Point, and Point Hueneme) house museums. Five California lighthouses, relocated from their original sites, now stand in new locations (Table Bluff, Cape Mendocino, Carquinez Straight, Southampton Shoals, and Oakland Harbor).

The great news is that many of the lighthouses in California have undergone restoration to some degree, and four are currently undergoing large restoration projects (St. George Reef, Point Sur, Piedras Blancas, and San Luis Obispo). The Bureau of Land Management operates Punta Gorda and Piedras Blancas. Point Montara and Pigeon Point are youth hostels, Oakland Harbor and Parkers' Lighthouse are restaurants, and East Brother and Point Cabrillo host bed and breakfasts. Piedras Blancas is home to a biology research station, and is an excellent resource for information on the history of this unique lighthouse.

The Long Beach Robot Light, built in 1949, would be the last major light constructed in California. A private aid to navigation rose at the entrance to the Long Beach Harbor 33 years later, as part of Parkers' Lighthouse Restaurant. In 2000, the "Rainbow Light," took shape as a conical tower, erected by the Long Beach Lyons Club, and located just across the harbor from Parkers' Lighthouse. In 2001, a community effort in Santa Cruz helped to build the Walton Lighthouse, located on the breakwater at the entrance to the harbor. None of these "lighthouses" has ever housed a light-keeper but actively guide ships as private aids to navigation.

Dedicated individuals involved in the preservation of these magnificent historical buildings strive to keep these distinctive structures intact for generations to come. We have entered a new era of the custodial maintenance of our lighthouses. Meanwhile, crews of volunteers strip away years of lead paint, remove well-meaning improvements, and painstakingly work to restore structures using original blueprints archived by the Federal Government. Thoughtful volunteers reintroduce native plants back into their rightful space. Obstacles to the protection of these architectural marvels are slowly being overcome. Much more work lies ahead to save the remaining lights, some in dangerously poor repair.

To those adventurous souls that yearn to visit the wonderful lighthouses of the golden state, please visit this books' companion web site www. CaLights.net where current links to official lighthouse web pages, more information on when to visit and how to get there can be found. Visit www. TheCanvasDigital.com where you can purchase additional copies of this book as well as my original artwork. This book has been a great education to me. It has allowed me the opportunity not only to visit these magnificent structures but also to explore the state and learn much of its history.

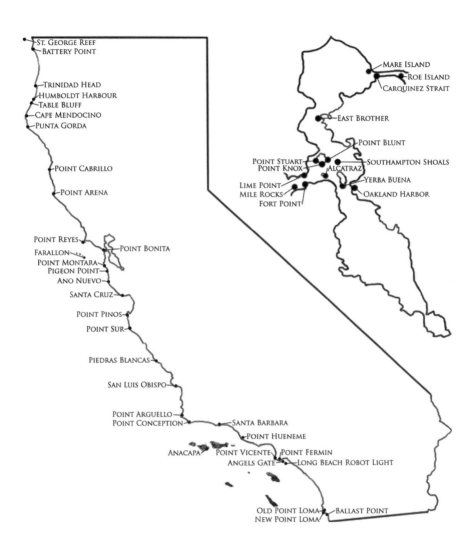

California lighthouse map
Drawing by Kent Weymouth

LIGHTING THE GOLD COAST!

At the close of 1846, San Francisco had a population of about 200 with some 90 buildings made up of frame houses, adobes, and shanties. In the entire year of 1847, six vessels entered San Francisco Bay. On the morning of January 24, 1848, James W. Marshall discovered gold in Coloma. By 1850, the population of San Francisco would soar to 36,154, more than one third of California's total population of 92,597. By 1854, the migration had reached 300,000. A quarter of those counted in California were foreigners. In San Francisco harbor, ships flew flags from England, Hamburg, France, Spain, Russia, Hawaii, Bremen, Portugal, Belgium, Sweden, Chile, Peru, Ireland, China, Italy, Mexico, Norway, and Tahiti. The ethnic diversity was unmatched anywhere on Earth, a trait that California carries on today.

The Sacramento and San Joaquin rivers were the transportation routes that linked San Francisco to the gold fields of California. This precipitated the need for lights to guide the ships through the various tributaries, past dangerous rocks, islands, and shoals. The San Francisco Bay region would eventually be home to the greatest concentration of lighthouses on the pacific coast. At one time or another within the bay, 16 lighthouses have been in operation, covering 100 miles of shoreline that encompass almost 450 square miles of inland waters. During the 1850s and 1860s, dozens of boats traveling the inland waterways transported passengers, mail, and freight. This was before 1869, when the Southern Pacific Railroad established business in the territory.

San Francisco 1848
Illustration courtesy of The United States Lighthouse Society

Lighthouse Administrations

The first Congress created the Lighthouse Service in 1789; then in 1820, supervision of the lighthouse system fell to the fifth auditor of the treasury. In August 1852, the United States Congress created the Lighthouse Board. The following October, the first meeting of the Lighthouse Board took place, discussing the task of maintaining the nation's lighthouses, lightships, buoys, fog signals, and aids to navigation. The Secretary of the Treasury filled the position of Board President, and to fill the board, President Andrew Johnson appointed three Navy officers, two scientists from the private sector, and three Army engineers. The Board decided to divide the nation into 12 districts, the twelfth made up of the entire west coast. An inspector assigned to each district was in charge of the daily operations of the personnel, with headquarters in San Francisco.

In April 1852, a contract to build the first eight lighthouses on the west coast for a total cost of $136,000 began between the government and Gibbons & Kelly. The lighthouses would be located at Humboldt Harbour, Southeast Farallon Island, Alcatraz Island, Fort Point (known then as Battery Point), Point Pinos, Point Conception, and Point Loma, as well as Cape Disappointment in Washington on the mouth of the Columbia River.

Gibbons & Kelly purchased the *Oriole*, as the supply ship to deliver the materials and men needed to build the west coast lighthouses. After the construction of Battery Point, Alcatraz, Point Pinos, and Southeast Farallon Island, the *Oriole* set sail for Cape Disappointment. Before arriving at her destination, the *Oriole* wrecked. No lives were lost, but the ship and cargo were a total loss. The wreck of the *Oriole* temporarily delayed Humboldt Harbour, Point Conception, and Point Loma. Southeast Farallon Island and Point Conception lighthouses had to be rebuilt because when the lenses arrived, they were too large to fit in the existing towers.

The use of local contractors rather than Gibbons & Kelly allowed the next eight lighthouses to undergo construction at a lower cost. During the Civil War, lighthouse construction ceased on the west coast, but in the decade following the war, 12 more lighthouses rose in California.

The Bureau of Lighthouses, created in 1910, replaced the Lighthouse Board, which had grown too large. The Board had operated by committee, but now, as part of the U.S. Commerce Department, one man, George Putnam, a civilian administrator with the Coast Survey, would head up the Bureau as Commissioner of Lighthouses. Appointed by President William Taft, Putnam would head the Bureau for 25 years and carry out the reorganization of the Lighthouse Service.

The administration of the Lighthouse Service was simplified, and district offices were combined. During these years documents become disorganized, convoluted, and less informative. Mechanization under the Bureau increased, through the application of modern devices and equipment that resulted in better aids to navigation and a gradual reduction in personnel, reducing operating costs. The Lighthouse Bureau handed over America's aids to navigation to the Coast Guard in 1939.

The Coast Guard chose Yerba Buena Island as the base for servicing lighthouses on the pacific coast from Northern Oregon to the Mexican Border. In 1943, a long-range electronic aid to navigation system, called Loran-A, (a system by which a ship or aircraft determines its position using radio signals sent out by two ground stations) began operation.

Large navigational buoys and the eventual use of solar power, would all work together toward the demise of the light-keeper, nicknamed "wickies." Unfortunately, the advent of automation and the lack of individuals on site also saw an increase of vandalism as well.

Lighthouse Superintendent's Conference - 1938
Photo courtesy of The United States Lighthouse Society

LIGHT-KEEPERS

The ability to read, write, and keep accurate records were the initial qualifications required to become a wickie. They had to be physically and mechanically able to maintain the buildings and equipment as well as make minor repairs. Their primary duties were to make sure that the light operated each night, and keep the fog signal in ready repair. At sunset, the keeper would fill the lamp reservoir with lard oil (later kerosene), then light the circular wick, allowing a good 30 minutes for the change in temperature before sliding the chimney over the wick, so the glass would not crack. A wickie, would light the lamp before dusk every night, at midnight trim the wick or change it for a fresh one, at dawn, extinguish the lamp, and draw the curtains before retiring.

Julia F. Williams - Santa Barbara Lighthouse Light-keeper 1865-1905
Photo courtesy of The United States Lighthouse Society

There were the usual jobs as well. Painting the station was part of the daily routine that always seemed to begin again just when the job was complete. Cleaning the brasswork in the lighthouse was a never-ending task. Maintaining the lantern room and lens was a particular chore. Inside the lens was a large reservoir, which needed continual filling with oil to fuel the beacon's lamp. The burner often needed to be changed or the wicks trimmed. Chores at a light station were abundant. Light keeping meant constant responsibility and working to stay ahead of the unrelenting abuse of the sea and salt air.

Many stations were tens of miles from the nearest town with little or no means of transportation, and in many locations there were no roads to travel on. Light-keepers, isolated by the physical location of the duty, also had a total lack of communication, before the advent of radio, television, or phones. Monotony and boredom were constant companions to those individuals residing at a lighthouse. To help quell the loneliness, as well as to stimulate the intellectual desires of these individuals, the Lighthouse Board established a portable rotating library in the 1880s that was circulated between lighthouses. These small wooden boxes housed approximately 50 books, including novels, books with topics of science, history and poetry as well as a prayer book and Bible. The scheduled tender would arrive with a new box, retrieving the old one for the next lighthouse. These rotating libraries were a welcome sight for residents, who devoured the books in an amazingly short period of time.

The United States also had a large number of female principal and assistant light-keepers, a practice that California carried on in many locations. Having a husband and wife team took place in the service, but more likely, a woman would be assigned to a location in the event of the death of her husband or father. California had many such women light-keepers; including Emily Fish at Point Pinos, Juliet Nichols at Angel Island, Laura Hecox at Santa Cruz, and Julia Williams at Santa Barbara.

Mrs. Theresa C. Watson and her daughter, Miss B. M. Watson and Kate C. McDougal were all appointed light-keepers at the Mare Island light.

THE LENS

The builders of the first lighthouses erected braziers or grates to house wood or coal fires, to use as their beacons for navigation. In 1763, the lighthouses in Liverpool England began using first sperm whale oil and then colza oil as the fuel source for flat wicks. Even the best parabolic lights had no real capability to be varied. The only significant change that could be made was to use colored glass, which diminished the intensity of the light from 25 to 40 percent.

In 1822, Augustin Fresnel constructed an annular lens using different rings receding from the axis in an attempt to eliminate any spherical aberration, with the bull's-eye being the only spherical component. These lenses, designed to replace the silvered reflectors previously used to intensify light, were intended for revolving lights only. The lens increased the distance the light could be visible and allowed for a variation or pattern to each light. In 1823, the first lighthouse to receive a Fresnel lens was the Cordouan lighthouse off the coast of France. Fresnel then designed a fixed and flashing light, which was produced by placing panels of straight refracting prisms in a vertical position on a revolving carriage outside the fixed light.

For the mariner, the ability to identify his location was a key component to navigation, and Fresnel's design allowed an easy means of identification. Multiple lenses of the same size, erected along the coast using individual characteristics, allowed a sailor to identify the lighthouse and the ships location.

A Fresnel lens was able to focus an oil lamp's rays further than ever before. To create a flash, the entire Fresnel lens had to rotate. This was achieved by placing the lens on either wheels or ball bearings in a track. At some stations, the lens floated in a bed of mercury, making it possible to turn a 6,000 pound lens with the gentle push of a finger.

Lighthouses using a clockwork mechanism to rotate the lens powered the device by a hanging weight, which rotated the carriage as the weight descended. The mechanism needed to be hand wound every two to eight hours, operating much like a grandfather clock.

In the late 1840s, the Lighthouse Service made the decision to use Fresnel lenses exclusively. Although construction had begun on Point Conception and Farallon Island, the towers, designed for a lamp and reflector were too small to accommodate the new Fresnel lenses, so the Lighthouse Service ordered the contractors to rebuild the towers. It took years to change parabolic reflectors to Fresnel lenses in other states, but perfect timing allowed California to stay ahead by having every lighthouse equipped with the latest technological advancement of the time.

E. Rosotte sculp   d'apres A. Tardieu

Augustin Fresnel - 1788-1827
Photo courtesy of The United States Lighthouse Society

The first order lens from St. George Reef Lighthouse on display at Del Norte Historical Society, Crescent City, CA. - Photograph by Kent Weymouth

STYLE

Unfamiliarity with the region prompted the Lighthouse Board to build the first seven lighthouses using a Cape Cod style that was a direct transplant from the shores of New England. The only remaining examples of this style are Point Pinos in Pacific Grove, San Diego's Old Point Loma, and Battery Point Lighthouse in Crescent City. The remaining five; Santa Barbara, the first Fort Point, the original Alcatraz, the first Point Bonita, and Humboldt Bay Harbour Light are all lost to history.

Initially no attempts to adapt architectural design to the needs of California were made. Soon however, earthquakes and extreme conditions on the California coast made lighthouse architects rethink their designs based on the geography, climate, and topography of the state.

Brick was the primary building material used in the first ten lighthouses constructed in California, but after 1856, other materials were favored. The tower at Point Arena was lost during the 1906 earthquake, requiring its demolition and replacement. The new Point Arena tower would be the first lighthouse in America to use reinforced concrete. Los Angeles Harbor, Point Vicente, Anacapa Island, Point Hueneme, Alcatraz, Point Arena, and Punta Gorda were all built of reinforced concrete and remain standing.

In Alaska, a new art-modern style of lighthouse built of reinforced concrete became the inspiration for the new lighthouse at Port Hueneme in 1942, making it the only art-modern lighthouse outside Alaska.

Cape Mendocino and Point Reyes lighthouses are constructed totally of iron, and Point Montara and Mile Rock used steel plates bolted together on site. Point Sur is one of two lighthouses built of stone; its stone quarried on site, while the other, St. George Reef Light, had its stone quarried on the mainland. New Point Loma, Año Nuevo, Point Arguello, and Fort Point had their lights installed atop metal skeleton structures.

Northern California, had an abundance of high quality redwood available at bargain prices. Fourteen of California's lighthouses used wood as their primary construction material, which proved to be inexpensive and readily available. Point Fermin and the original Point Hueneme, built at the same time, used the same plans, and both began operation on the same day in 1874. Santa Cruz, Mare Island, and East Brother shared similar styles. Of these, only East Brother exists today. Ballast Point, San Luis Obispo, and Table Bluff used nearly identical plans. Point Cabrillo, the Roe Island lighthouse, Oakland Harbor, and Southampton Shoals used an arts and crafts style in their construction. Point Vicente and Anacapa Island light stations used design adopting the locally popular Spanish Revival. The elegant neoclassic style of the Carquinez Lighthouse is unique and the tower at Yerba Buena Island is the only one of its kind.

Battery Point Lighthouse
Photograph by Kent Weymouth

Point Fermin Lighthouse
Photo courtesy of The United States Lighthouse Society

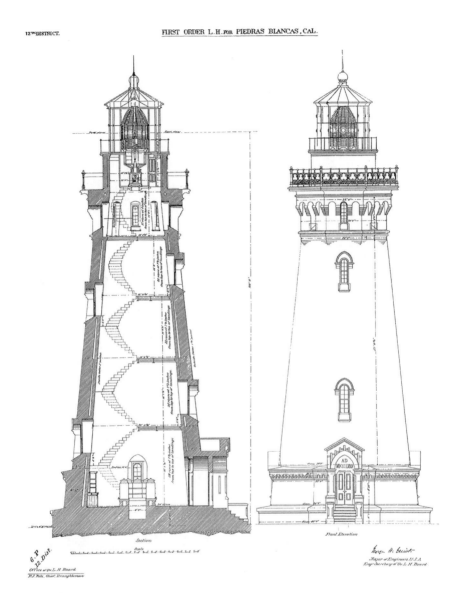

Piedras Blancas Light Station
Image courtesy of The Bureau of Land Management

LIGHTING THE SOUTH

OLD POINT LOMA

There is no preparation for the magnificent view that awaits visitors to the Cabrillo National Monument. The statue of the explorer Juan Cabrillo, his arms outreached, presents a view of the ocean that envelopes the monument on three sides of this glorious extended point. To the south lays Mexico, to the east, San Diego Harbor and the shimmering skyline of San Diego. To the west lies the great expanse of the Pacific Ocean. The finger of land in the bay to the northwest was home to the Ballast Point Lighthouse, although nothing remains of the old light or the compound. Behind the statue of Cabrillo is the monument gift shop, as well as an auditorium that presents programs on the Pacific Grey Whale and Juan Rodriguez Cabrillo, the first European to discover San Diego. On the crest of the hill to the west is the Old Point Loma lighthouse. The New Point Loma Light Station is an active military post and inaccessible to the public, but can be seen from the end of the walkway behind the Old Point Loma Lighthouse.

Three of California's original seven lighthouses remain intact; Old Point Loma, Battery Point in Crescent City and Point Pinos in Monterey have all been beautifully restored. These stations are kept in historically accurate form and are great examples of lighthouse preservation.

During California's Spanish rule, from 1542 to 1821, settlers built signal fires at Point Loma to guide supply vessels into the harbor. John Drake Sloat, Commander and Chief to the Pacific Squadron received orders in 1846 to claim the west coast for the United States, should war break out between America and Mexico. So when reports of Mexico's attack on the Texas border came, Sloat set sail. On July 7, 1846, Commodore Sloat, raised the American flag in Monterey, mid July would see the American flag flying over every port in California.

After the Mexican American war, the Guadalupe Hidalgo treaty, signed in 1846, made California the property of the United States of America. When California entered the union, the coastal survey chose Point Loma as one of the first seven locations on the California coast to receive a navigational aid.

The construction company Gibbons & Kelly, had not actually surveyed the area before submitting the bid to build the lighthouse, and initially balked at the location of the light and objected to the monumental logistical challenges of the job. The Lighthouse Board offered the opportunity to withdraw from the construction but noted that a withdrawal from Point Loma would also mean the withdrawal of Gibbons and Kelly from any other lighthouse contracts awarded them on the west coast. Gibbons and Kelly relented and went immediately to work. Since no road was in place, a crew of 18 men took 35 days to complete a road that would be used to carry the materials needed up to the construction site.

The lighthouse, built in the same cottage style as all of California's first lights, used locally quarried rock brought from Ballast Point, along with materials transported aboard the steamer Vaquero from San Francisco. Floor tiles from the old Spanish Fort Guijarros previously located on Ballast Point became part of the new lighthouse. Plans to use a first order Fresnel lens proved problematic when the tower was too small to accommodate the lens. In its place, a fixed third order lens intended for Humboldt Bay became the light at Point Loma. On the evening of November 15, 1855, the first keeper climbed the stairs of the 46-foot tower and lit the lamp for

Old Point Loma Lighthouse
Photo courtesy of The United States Lighthouse Society

the first time.

The station was cramped and isolated. The building's four rooms housed the light-keeper, assistant light-keeper, and their families. In 1876, the assistant light-keeper and his family received one more room by splitting the woodshed in half, which became their dwelling for quite some time, although totally unsuitable for a home.

As Point Loma Lighthouse entered 1891, it still held the distinction of being the light at the greatest elevation in the United States. When making the choice for the location, the peak of the point had seemed the logical choice, allowing one light to do the job of covering the bay and the ocean, but in hindsight, the light stood at an elevation often obscured by a thick fog that would roll in from the pacific. The Lighthouse Board decided to relocate the lighthouse to below the fog line with a pair of lights. The first to open was the Ballast Point Light Station in 1890, followed by the New Point Loma Light Station in 1891. After 36 years in operation, the light at Old Point Loma went dark in March 1891.

The original buildings, damaged by souvenir hunters and vandals, fell into such a deplorable state of disrepair that the assistant keeper's dwelling and other buildings were razed.

In 1913, President Woodrow Wilson signed a proclamation making the property containing the Old Point Loma lighthouse a National Monument. From 1913 to 1933 responsibility for the lighthouse fell to the United States Army; it was during this time that the soldiers were encouraged to live in, and make small repairs or restorations to the old buildings to help prevent further decay.

Franklin D. Roosevelt transferred the Cabrillo National Monument from the War Department to the National Park system in 1933 and the lighthouse became designated as part of the Cabrillo National Monument. Using drawings, all available records, and interpretation of existing aspects, restoration began.

During World War II, Cabrillo National Monument closed, and the lighthouse was painted green to serve as a Navy signal tower. In 1946, the National Park Service resumed control of the monument. The fourth order Fresnel lens from the Table Bluff Lighthouse, found a home at Old Point Loma in 1955 during a celebration of the 100th anniversary of the lighthouse. During a major restoration in 1984, the third order lens from Mile Rocks replaced the previous lens.

Every evening the light from Old Point Loma beams out from the hilltop, so not to confuse ships at sea, it is visible from the Bay side only. A replica of the assistant keeper's residence stands as a museum, housing the lens (restored in 2002) removed from the New Point Loma lighthouse.

New Point Loma

New Point Loma Light Station
Photo courtesy of The United States Lighthouse Society

Even before the construction of the Old Point Loma Lighthouse began, there were concerns that fog might envelop the light if it rested on the point at such a great elevation. The precognition would prove to be right. After only 36 years in operation, the old lighthouse was decommissioned and replaced with two lights to do the job that the Lighthouse Board had hoped could be accomplished by one. On the Bay side, Ballast Point began operation in 1890, and the New Point Loma Light on Pelican Point came to life on March 23, 1891. The old lighthouse, abandoned and no longer maintained, soon fell into disrepair.

The new lighthouse station consisted of the metal framework tubular tower, two Victorian cottages, a cistern, a barn, and a privy. The tower arrived via two flatcars, in early July 1890, and came from Old Town to the point on wagons. Unlike any other tower on the west coast, an interior walkway allowed access to the lamp, with a second walkway surrounding the cupola. The entire lighthouse was constructed of cast iron throughout, except for the wrought iron tension rods on the tower frame.

So proud of the Fresnel lens he had made for the new lighthouse at Point Loma, Henri Le Paute wanted to enter it in the Paris Exhibition of 1889. The lens won a gold medal, prompting Le Paute to request permission to exhibit the lens at Chicago's Colombian Exposition in 1893. The Lighthouse Service agreed and obtained a replacement lens to install in its place, which turned out to be too large, so the service procured a different lens to complete the tower. After winning another prize at the Colombian Exhibition, the Lighthouse Board decided rather than ship the lens back to Point Loma they would install the lens in the new Chicago Harbor Lighthouse, which was opening at the same time as the closing of the Colombian Exhibition.

A fog signal, established in March 1913, was installed directly behind the metal tower. Radio beacons arrived in the 1920s followed by the advent of electricity, which came to the light in 1933. A black-out order, imposed on the station during World War II extinguished the light in the tower, requiring the keepers to place black tarpaper over the windows when using interior lights. The station changed its color during the war, when the dwellings, the lighthouse, the outbuildings, and even the sidewalks were painted an olive drab. Automation came to the New Point Loma station in 1973.

The tower was starting to show signs of deterioration due to corrosion in 1996, the watch room floor was not level, and the lens no longer rotated smoothly on the chariot mechanism. When the Fresnel lens became inoperable, a Vega Rotating Beacon took its place. The ultimate aim became restoring the optic assembly to a fully operable condition, but in December 2002, after 111 years, the Fresnel lens retired from the New Point Loma lantern room.

In 2005, Cabrillo National Monument put the lens on display in a replica of the assistant keeper's cottage built near the Old Point Loma Lighthouse.

New Point Loma Lighthouse is on Coast Guard property and is not open to the public. The station is visible from behind the Old Point Loma Lighthouse at the end of the walkway.

BALLAST POINT

Nothing remains of the lighthouse compound that used to reside on this outcropping of land now used by the United States Navy as a submarine base. Off limits to civilians, this outpost holds no signs of its past lighthouse history.

Sebastian Vizcaino named the harbor "San Diego" in 1602, and Ballast Point was named by the seamen who sailed flat bottom vessels along the coast. The stones collected from the point were used as ballast on ships sailing north, and then sold in Sacramento for $20 a ton as street pavers. The Spaniards used the point as a stake light to warn the ships of Spain and Mexico.

The United States Government established Ballast Point as a harbor light in 1890. Stretching out into the entrance of San Diego Bay like a huge thumb, Ballast Point extends from Point Loma midway between the ocean and the bay. The compound consisted of the keeper's dwelling, which also housed the lighthouse tower, a dwelling for an assistant, and a fog-bell house. The Victorian structure housed a fifth order Fresnel lens, and used the same design as the light at San Luis Obispo, lit the same year.

The responsibility of the two keepers was to maintain the station light, as well as nine beacons, two fog-signals, four gas-buoys, the buildings, wharf, launch and road. In addition to these tasks, the keepers also stood watch, six hours on, and six hours off.

Several times a week one of the keepers would make a run up and

Ballast Point Lighthouse
Photo courtesy of The United States Lighthouse Society

Ballast Point Lighthouse
Photo courtesy of The United States Lighthouse Society

down the bay, and on occasion out into the ocean to re-light the "gas buoy" or whistling-buoy. Exiting the bay in poor weather was no small task, and bad weather was often the cause for the light to go out. It was necessary to get it re-lit as quickly as possible for the safety of the men of the sea. It was quite a feat, to get from the launch to the buoy, find a firm footing on the wet metal, and then cling on with one hand while re-lighting the buoy with the other.

The fog-bell had to be re-wound every hour when in use and kept the men on their toes. If the mechanism failed to function, the men would ring the bell by hand, swinging the huge clapper against the side of the bell once a minute. In 1960, new modern equipment replaced the lighthouse and fog signal building, the property was razed, and the point reclassified as a "Light Attendant Station." In December 1970, the station became an unmanned secondary light.

Long Beach Robot Light

The Long Beach Robot Light, located on the San Pedro middle breakwater, is just a short distance from the Angel's Gate Lighthouse. This structure, built on a base of six concrete columns incased in iron pipe, has begun to deteriorate, the iron pipe is pulling back from the cement it once surrounded. This rectangular art deco building supports a smaller square box on top, surmounted with a light.

Built in 1949, to withstand earthquakes and seismic tidal waves, the Robot Light originally had two generators supplying power to the light and foghorn that were fueled automatically from a reservoir in the base of the lighthouse.

Time and the elements have not been kind to this structure. Large chunks of cement have come out of the outer sea facing wall. The Coast Guardsmen from the Aids to Navigation Team do not enter this structure unless necessary, as the structural integrity is unknown. The automated beacon sits on top of this simple structure. As plain as this light is, it is a beautiful building with a unique and distinct style that adds an interesting character to the breakwater. Always automated, this light has never housed a crew or light-keeper and was originally controlled from the Angels Gate Lighthouse. Long Beach Harbor is strictly a commercial port, no ocean liners, sport, or recreational vessels enter here, and with the loading docks filled with thousands of containers stacked along the pier, the Long Beach Robot Light goes virtually unseen. It would be wonderful to see this light restored, but the Long Beach Robot Light may be the California lighthouse in the greatest danger of being lost.

Long Beach Robot Light
Photograph by Kent Weymouth

L. A. HARBOR (ANGELS GATE)

The first southern California land boom took place between 1881 and 1887, when the population of Los Angeles grew from 10,000 to 70,000. The increasing commerce moving in and out of the Wilmington harbor required a light and fog-signal for safety. Completed in 1910, consisting of almost three million tons of rock, the 9,250-foot long breakwater, built to protect the Los Angeles and Long Beach Harbors from huge damaging waves, would be the home of the new Angels Gate Lighthouse. Poured at the end of the breakwater, a concrete foundation, consisting of a 40-foot square cement pad would act as the lighthouse foundation. After the pad had cured, the concrete block endured storms for one year before construction of the superstructure began.

The San Pedro Harbor Light, also known as Angels Gate, came to life for the first time on March 1, 1913. Standing 69-feet tall, Angels Gate sits in 51-feet of water, and has a style truly unlike any other lighthouse ever built.

The base of this three story Romanesque lighthouse, built around 12 steel columns is octagonal. The second story is dodecagonal, and the third, fourth and fifth stories are cylindrical. The lower floor contained the fog-signal machinery, water and fuel tanks, and water supply pumps.

A swinging boom derrick used a hoisting engine to handle heavy articles, lifting the station launch to and from the boat cradle. Supplies, brought from San Pedro were landed on the breakwater by boat or in the keepers' launch. The illuminating apparatus consisted of a fourth order bivalve flashing Fresnel lens, revolving on ball bearings driven by clockworks. Angel's Gate had quarters for three keepers, while their families lived on shore.

A violent storm struck the Los Angeles area in 1939, and for five days the sea came rolling over the breakwater, sending the waves crashing against the tower with monumental force. The great tower, built into the monolithic block of concrete, repeatedly pounded with seawater appeared to stand tall. Shutters, securely closed, kept out the ocean, and the tower stood resolute from the force of the oncoming tide. After the storm had passed, one of keepers mentioned that it took much more effort for him to walk in one direction inside the building than the other. His fellow coasties were not so convinced, so he dared them to try the same experiment. When they tried it themselves, he appeared to be right, but they needed more proof. The men went out onto the lighthouse gallery, and dropped a plumb line to the towers base. They revealed that the entire tower now had a tilt leaning toward the shore with a decided easterly list. The lean has been accentuated by years of rust, earthquakes, storms, and on at least one occasion, being struck by a ship. The punishment that this structure

Angels Gate Lighthouse
Photo courtesy of The United States Lighthouse Society

has endured for almost 100 years is proof that the lighthouse was a true masterpiece of engineering. Very few structures have been built that could have withstood the ongoing punishment of the unrelenting sea.

Storms often meant constant confinement of the crew until the danger passed, sometimes marooning keepers for an entire week at a time. The crew ran out of fuel on one such occasion, even though an ample supply was located in the storage house located just yards away. No man dared to step foot from the tower, so dangerous were the breaking seas. The cook was forced to prepare meals using a blowtorch. Storm shutters tore off the tower, and windows were shattered 35-feet above normal water. As always, the lighthouse stood resolute.

In 1942, during World War II, the U.S. Navy built a degaussing station and a radio direction finding calibration unit. Navy personnel, who worked on this equipment, lived in a two-story concrete dwelling constructed just outside the tower.

One evening, a light-keeper, jarred from his chair by the sound of grinding steel against rock, saw the running lights of a giant battleship as it scraped by. The huge grey ship had struck the jetty as it entered the harbor, bouncing it back into the channel. The battleship made it to the harbor with only a few scratches, but the keeper was a nervous wreck for a week. The event remained sealed in the Navy Department's confidential files for many years.

The deep two-tone foghorn, affectionately known to the locals as "Moaning Maggie" retired in 1952, and was replaced by a high-pitched single-tone horn, referred to as "Blatting Betty" which was disliked by local mariners.

In September 1966, severe storm warnings took place along the southern California coast, with a forecast for 12-foot waves. At San Pedro, the waves were washing over the top of the breakwater. The lighthouse had watertight doors, but the bottom floor had often flooded during past storms. Next to the tower stood the adjacent Navy quarters building, with the storage building located farther down the breakwater. To prevent water damage, it was routine procedure to raise everything off the floor onto the highest shelves in these buildings before a storm. After completing this task on one such occasion, Engineers Mate third class Kent Knierim, Seaman David Aikens, and Seaman Apprentice Richard "Mike" Miles, along with the station mascot, a black German shepherd named King, began to cross the breakwater back to the lighthouse from the storage building. It was 9 p.m., and while Knierim, Aikens and King started back through the spray, Miles stayed back to light a cigarette, using the wall of the storage building as a windbreak. When Knierim and Aikens had almost reached the lighthouse tower, Knierim said to Aikens, "Look at this wave coming!" Aikens turned around just in time to see a wall of water four to five-feet high sweeping across the top of the breakwater. The wave caught Aikens and threw him into the steel wires of the breakwater lifelines. Caught for a moment by the throat and the chest, Aikens was stunned, and in a flash, he washed over the side of the breakwater and into the harbor. Knierim had more time to react to the wave, but as he lunged for the lifelines, the wave hit. He was slammed head first into one of the steel posts; thankfully, he was wearing a metal hard hat that absorbed the blow. Swept through the lifelines, Knierim grabbed onto one of the posts and was left dangling just above the rocks and waves, until help could arrive. Shielded from the wave by the paint and storage building, Miles watched in horror as his crew mates washed overboard. As the water receded, Miles saw Knierim's hand clutching onto the post. After helping Knierim back onto the breakwater platform, Miles ran inside the lighthouse and grabbed two life jackets. Knierim removed his raincoat and boots and began to scan the water for Aikens, who was a poor swimmer at best. When Miles saw Aikens bob to the surface briefly and disappear, he threw him a life jacket, passing the second to Knierim, who stuffed the life jacket under his arm and climbed over the lifelines. Knierim leapt into the crest of a wave and swam towards Aikens. After reaching him, Knierim tried to drag Aikens back toward the lighthouse, but the current was too strong. Both found themselves swept toward the harbor entrance and into the open sea. At the lighthouse, Miles contacted the nearby Coast Guard Station at Terminal Island. Luckily, the search and rescue boat was beginning a routine harbor patrol. Miles returned to the scene, and as the two men drifted away, he kept a flashlight beam focused on them to direct the Coast Guard boat, which arrived only five minutes later and quickly pulled the cold and exhausted men from the water. Both Aikens and Knierim asked the crew of the boat to search for their dog King, but after Aikens began to complain of chest pains, the search was called off. Transported to a hospital ship moored at Long Beach Naval Base, Aikens and Knierim remained for observation.

The evening of the event after everyone was gone; Miles heard a strange noise above the sound of the raging storm that was coming from the entrance of the tower. Frightened by this bizarre development, he nevertheless went down stairs to find out what it was. At the door was King, the station mascot, dripping wet with his tail tucked between his legs, his body trembling. Miles brought the poor dog inside where it hid in the nearest closet and remained there the whole next day, continuing to quiver. Somehow, King had survived being swept off the pier into the ocean and had made his way back to the lighthouse through the gale. David Aikens spent a few days in the hospital suffering with broken ribs. Kent Knierim, treated for minor injuries and released, later received a Coast Guard Life Saving Medal for his rescue, and Mike Miles received a Letter of Commendation. King recovered and continued to serve at the lighthouse alongside his crew of Coasties.

In February 1973, automation of the Angels Gate Lighthouse was complete and the keepers left the tower. Solar panels, set in place, made Angels Gate the first lighthouse on the west coast powered by solar generated batteries. The green light of Angels Gate has become a hallmark of Los Angeles, distinguishing it from other West Coast ports. The original fourth order lens is on display at Los Angeles Maritime Museum in San Pedro.

POINT FERMIN

High atop the southernmost point of the Palos Verdes peninsula sits Point Fermin, one of the most accessible lighthouse structures in California. Completely restored and beautifully landscaped, with lush surroundings and manicured lawns, the lighthouse sits on a federal reservation within Point Fermin City Park.

British explorer George Vancouver named Point Fermin for Father Fermin Francisco de Lasuen, Padre Presidente of California, who established nine of the twenty-one Alta California missions. The gesture was in appreciation of the hospitality shown to him by Father Fermin at the mission in Carmel.

In June 1872, the U.S. Congress made appropriations to build a lighthouse at Point Fermin, selecting a site at the top of a 100-foot cliff overlooking the ocean. The 37 acres of land needed for the reservation was in the hands of multiple owners, and the U.S. Government plans to purchase the land were unsuccessful. Therefore, condemnation proceedings began, ending successfully in favor of the government in November 1873. Jose Diego Sepulveda graciously donated the three-acre pad of land required for the lighthouse to the government. In order to make the transaction legal, Sepulveda was paid $35.00, but he returned the check, which is on record in Wilmington.

Paul J. Pelz, a well-known and respected drafter and architect for the Lighthouse Board, had designed the building that houses the Library of Congress, the St. Augustine Lighthouse, as well as many others before

Point Fermin Lighthouse
Photo courtesy of The United States Lighthouse Society

designing the Point Fermin Lighthouse. Gabled roofs characterized the "stick style" Victorian construction used. Horizontal siding, decorative crossbeams and hand carved porch railings accented this ornate structure. The Point Fermin Lighthouse was built using redwood lumber brought by ship from the forests of northern California, and topped with a cupola that housed a fourth order Fresnel lens brought around Cape Horn. The original Port Hueneme lighthouse, located in Oxnard, used the same elegant design.

There was no source of water found on the Point Fermin headland, so provisions for collecting rain began. Large troughs used in place of conventional gutters could handle the volume of water generated by the heaviest downpour. Connected by a manifold system, the water ran to the three cisterns located along the eastern edge of the lighthouse, about 20-yards or so from the structure. The cisterns, constructed out of bricks, had a cement-coated lining; a windmill pumped the water from the cisterns to the residents.

December 15, 1874, Point Fermin began operation. The first light-keeper was Mary L. Smith who held the post until May 1882, with the help and companionship of her sister Helen. The sisters had moved to San Pedro because they thought the climate would be healthy. Their brother Victor was a Washington Territory customs officer and was undoubtedly influential in helping them to obtain their positions.

The sisters maintained the light for eight years on what was at the time, a barren, isolated headland. The nearest settlers were in Wilmington, over six miles away. The Smiths finally concluded it was too lonely for them and retired from the Lighthouse Service.

James Herald became the second light-keeper at Point Fermin but did not remain at the station for very long. Herald was replaced by Captain George Shaw, who lived at Point Fermin as light-keeper with his wife and daughter for 22 years. Captain Shaw was the first light-keeper at Point Fermin to wear the U.S. Lighthouse Service uniform. Women were not required to wear the uniform that became mandatory of all male Lighthouse Service employees in 1884.

Visiting the lighthouse was an event. A buggy trip to Point Fermin even from San Pedro took half a day. Regular boat trips brought visitors from Long Beach to San Pedro where they would board the trolley for the final leg of their trip. Many visitors took the Red Car, and walked the short distance to the lighthouse. Other people came by horse and buggy, and later by automobile. An average of 3 thousand people visited the lighthouse yearly.

William Lewis Austin served as light-keeper at Point Arena and Point Conception, before moving into the Point Fermin lighthouse in 1917. Austin, the father of six children, filled the lighthouse for the first time with children. When both William and Martha Austin passed away in 1925, the occupation of light-keeper fell to their oldest daughter Thelma Austin. Thelma would become the last light-keeper of Point Fermin, as well as gaining the responsibility of raising the four children remaining at home.

"When my parents died over a year ago, my sister Juanita and I were determined to carry on the work which my parents started. My dear father had been a lighthouse keeper for many years; in fact, I was brought into the lighthouse atmosphere when but three years of age, when my father accepted the commission to tend the lighthouse at Point Arena on the Pacific coast. My sister was born there. And we were both reared in that romantic environment so you can readily see that it is our very life.

When I was growing into young womanhood, my father accepted the post of light-keeper at Point Conception one of the most isolated points on the Pacific Coast and here I experienced many marine disasters. I will never forget that terrible night when I experienced my first shipwreck, when the lumber freighter "Shasta" went on the rocks and was slowly dashed to pieces. Although the sight sort of chilled me, I derived a grim satisfaction nevertheless from the knowledge that my dear Father was doing everything within his power to save the crew... Then in 1917 my father accepted the commission to tend the lighthouse here at Point Fermin, so we moved immediately taking up our duty. There is something very sentimental about this old lighthouse, for both father and mother somehow felt that this was their most important post, since father really was pioneering here. And he came to be loved and admired by all the old seamen passing in and out of Los Angeles harbor.

When my mother died a little over a year ago, my father just seemed to waste away. In fact, he died of a broken heart, since they had been together all these years in the lighthouse work, and my sister and I felt that we had a sacred duty to perform: to promulgate the heroic work which our parents started... to make my burden the harder to bear, my baby sister married a sailor, leaving me alone here to 'carry on'. If you would have associated with lighthouses and the sea as much as I have, you would know that I never could get lonesome as long as the pounding of the breakers is audible, and the ocean liners continue to sail past my door. And instead of growing monotonous and tiresome, the regular routine about the lighthouse seems a source of great comfort to me."

Woman's World, August 1929

Thelma would remain as keeper until 1927, when management of the light turned over to the Department of Recreation and Parks. The lighthouse would become the residence for the Park Foreman, who would also tend the light. Oscar Johnson who lived at Point Fermin with his wife was the last man to tend the station, extinguishing the light at Point Fermin for the last time on December 6, 1941.

On December 7, 1941, after the attack on Pearl Harbor, coastal lights went dark as a precaution against enemy attack. Point Fermin was closed to the public for the duration of the war. Painted a green camouflage to hide the lighthouse from enemy pilots, the building also had the lantern housing, railings, revolving lens, and mechanism removed. Installed on the site was a battery of searchlights, and constructed on the tower, a crude wooden type of shelter dubbed "the chicken coop," accommodated a radar lookout station maintained for the duration of the war.

The Army's plan at the beginning of the war was to remove the Fresnel lens, along with all related equipment, and store it on the premises for the duration, returning the light after the war. The U.S. Navy set up residence at the lighthouse during the war and used it as a lookout tower and signaling station. Because of the demands for space, someone decided to transfer all of these things to the storage yard at the Coast Guard Base on Terminal Island.

When the war was over, the lens had somehow disappeared, so out of necessity or perhaps just practicality, an automatic beacon was established on the outer point in late 1945. Once stripped of all electronic equipment, the lighthouse once again turned over to the Department of Recreation and Parks. The intervening years were not kind to Point Fermin, as it began to deteriorate and become an eyesore.

In 1969, the San Pedro community took the first steps to create a Point Fermin Lighthouse restoration committee. Two dedicated citizens, Bill Olesen and John Olguin, raised funds and worked diligently to replace the lantern room and the lighthouse to its original glory. Their efforts also placed the lighthouse on the National Register of Historic Places in 1973. In 2002, Point Fermin underwent a $2.6 million restoration. A new lantern gallery, replicated from the original design was also included. In 2003, Point Fermin Lighthouse, one of San Pedro's most recognized landmarks, reopened to the public using volunteers from the Point Fermin Lighthouse Society as tour guides.

After a long exhaustive search, the Point Fermin lens was found in late 2006. After bringing in specialists to confirm the lens origin, it was returned to its home at Point Fermin.

POINT VICENTE

Point Vicente Light Station
Photo courtesy of The United States Lighthouse Society

Point Vicente is located on the most prominent point of the Palos Verdes Peninsula between Point Loma and Point Conception. When approaching in foggy weather there is practically no warning of its presence to the sailor until the cliff suddenly appears. At the beginning of the twentieth century, there was an unlighted gap of 32 nautical miles on the usual courses taken between Point Hueneme Light Station and Point Fermin Light Station. All steamer traffic on the Pacific Ocean south of San Francisco both foreign and domestic had to pass by this point, where the 100 fathom curve lies within one half mile of the shore. With the opening of the Panama Canal in 1907, freight and passenger traffic would increase exponentially along this part of the coast.

Masters and ship-owners signed petitions to establish a flashing light and first-class fog signal at Point Vicente. The original plan was to discontinue the Point Fermin light upon completion of Point Vicente. Conventional thinking was Point Fermin would no longer be required with lights at both San Pedro Harbor (Angels Gate), and Point Vicente. In actuality, the Point Fermin Lighthouse would remain in service until 1941.

The buildings, built of a frame construction in a Spanish revival style, have a stucco finish and red tile roofing. Vicente's reinforced concrete tower and lantern room stand 67-feet tall. After 40 years of service, the third order lens from Sitka, Alaska began a new life on April 14, 1926, when the U.S. Lighthouse Service began the operation of Point Vicente. The lens was mounted on a low structural steel pedestal placed directly on the floor of the lantern room, and rotated on a heavy ball race, driven through a worm gear by an electric motor.

During the war, black-out curtains hung in all the windows, the lamp was reduced to 25 watts, and watch patrols were set up along the shore. After the war, the rotating beam became a disturbance to local residents and a hazard to motorists on Palos Verdes drive. Light-keepers painted the inside of the lantern house windows on the land side with a coat of white paint to end the annoyance.

In 1971, electronic sensors to activate the foghorn were set in place and automation came to the lighthouse at Point Vicente. In November 1979, Point Vicente Lighthouse became part of the National Registry of Historic Sites. Still an active USCG base, the housing facility is home to Coast Guard Commanding Officers from Integrated Support Command at San Pedro.

Point Vicente Light Station
Photo courtesy of The United States Lighthouse Society

Point Hueneme

The dangerous Santa Barbara Channel had became the resting place of more than 33 shipwrecks between 1849 and 1900, the most famous was the *Winfield Scott* a 225-foot long side-wheel steamer. An American eagle with a coat of arms was mounted on her stern, and her bow was adorned with a bust carved in the likeness of General Winfield Scott. When properly loaded, the steamer had accommodations for 165 cabin and 150 steerage passengers with a dining saloon that could serve 100 people.

The *Winfield Scott* departed San Francisco upon its last voyage in December 1853, with a full load of passengers and a shipment of $2 million in gold bullion. In an effort to save time, Captain Simon F. Blunt decided to use the Santa Barbara Channel rather than the usual passage outside the islands. As the ship entered the passage, fog began to roll in. Blunt intended to steam between Anacapa and Santa Cruz Islands, but instead, the *Winfield Scott* struck Middle Anacapa Island at full speed.

According to the *Winfield Scott Vessel History* obtained from the *Channel Islands National Marine Sanctuary*; Edward Bosqui was a passenger on the ill-fated ship and recalled the events of that evening.

"At midnight I was suddenly awakened from a sound sleep by a terrible jar and crashing of timbers. Tumbling out of my berth, I was confronted by the horror stricken visage of my toothless and bald-headed stateroom companion, who had not time to secure his wig and false teeth and was groping about to find them. Leaving him paralyzed with fear, I hurried out on deck, where my attention was fixed on a wall of towering cliffs, the tops of which were hidden by the fog and darkness and appeared about to fall and crush us. All round was the loud booming of angry breakers surging about invisible rocks."

The fortunate passengers survived the ordeal by having an island on which to spend the night. The following day the side-wheel steamer *California* picked up most of the women and children. For the men, their stay on the island would last eight days until the *California* returned, provisioned and ready to continue to Panama. Some of the crew remained to recover mail and passenger baggage still submerged in the hull.

Point Hueneme Light Station
Photo courtesy of The United States Lighthouse Society

The *Winfield Scott* was a total loss and the shipwreck started a serious push to have a lighthouse built in the area to aid navigation.

Captain Horatio Gates Trussell of Santa Barbara salvaged the wreck, and used the wood he saved in his home, which is now preserved as the Trussell-Winchester Adobe by the Santa Barbara Historical Society. The home also contains two brass thresholds from the ship.

With cliffs that rise out of the water 250-feet, Anacapa Island was the ideal location for a light to warn ships at sea, but the island posed many obstacles to building a lighthouse on its soil. A tower eventually built on Anacapa in 1912, would give way in 1932, to the last lighthouse built in California, but in 1874, a lighthouse on Anacapa was prohibitive. The island sits 12 miles off a point called Hueneme (pronounced "Wy-nee-mee" from the Chumash Indian word meaning "half-way" or "resting place") on the eastern entrance to the Santa Barbara Channel.

Only ten-feet above sea level, the lighthouse was built with a combination of Swiss and Elizabethan style, and used the same plan as Point Fermin 53 miles to the southeast. The lighthouse, a two-story, ten-room house with a second-story balcony, four fireplaces, three chimneys, a front porch and a square 65-foot tower that rose from the middle of the structure, presented a dignified appearance to the 14 acre light station.

Lit on December 15, 1874, the same day as Point Fermin, Hueneme used a lard-oil lamp to supply the light for the fourth order Fresnel. The weights to turn the Fresnel lens ran through a pipe in the bathroom.

The first floor housed the head keeper and his family while the second story was for the assistant and his family. The well-maintained grounds served as a small park complete with benches, shrubs, beautiful lawns, flower beds and a fishpond. Eventually the grounds were flooded, and destroyed by high seas. A fog signal was added to the station in 1882.

Charles F. Allen began his career with the Lighthouse Service in 1892, as assistant light-keeper at the Humboldt Harbour Lighthouse and Table Bluff Lighthouse. Appointed the light-keeper at the Point Hueneme Lighthouse in 1894, afforded both of the Allen children the opportunity to be born in lighthouses. The eldest, Mrs. John W. Mahan was born at the old North Spit lighthouse and Miss Melba, the youngest, was born at Hueneme. Allen was an inventor who was always at work on some mechanical contrivance to facilitate the running of laborsaving machinery. In his life he invented and patented a beet plow, a steam turbine, an ore crusher, an amalgamator, a concentrator, a water wheel superior to others in use, an improved drive well, and numerous other smaller inventions. He also made improvements on driving gears for automobiles, invented a new steel-clad pneumatic automobile tire, and made various improvements on bicycles and automobiles. After 20 years of service at Hueneme, Charles F. Allen resigned and started a hay baling business.

In 1928, Richard Bard created a new county-wide harbor district with the goal of dredging a port at Hueneme. Just off Hueneme was a deep-water canyon that would now serve as the entrance to the new harbor. The harbor, built precariously close to the 66-year-old lighthouse, made relocation of the structure necessary. The structure sold for the sum of $51 to the harbor commission with the intention of turning the structure into a facility for the Yacht Club, to be located on the west jetty of the new harbor. In 1940, Point Hueneme became the first lighthouse in history relocated from its original site. Placed on a barge, Point Hueneme Lighthouse was moved across the channel in preparation for the new harbor construction. Two years later, the Navy took over the harbor. Space being an important commodity during the war prompted the removal of the original structure. The lens, lantern, and clockwork mechanism were moved to a temporary tower.

The new 48-foot-high square tower built in an art modern style began its life in 1941, fitted with a fourth order lens. The tower sits upon its own fog signal building and its light can be visible for 22 miles under the right conditions. Automated in 1972, the fourth order Fresnel lens made by Barbier & Benard in 1897, is still in operation today. Owned and operated by the U.S. Coast Guard, the lighthouse is located on the USCG station at Port Hueneme and only opens to the public one day a month.

ANACAPA ISLAND

Part of the Channel Islands National Park, Anacapa is actually made up of three islands. East Anacapa Island is home to the Anacapa Lighthouse and measures a quarter of a mile wide and one mile long, with cliffs rising 250-feet above sea level. Middle Anacapa is a quarter of a mile wide and one and a half miles long, with an elevation of 325-feet at its highest point. Western Anacapa is the largest of the three islands, measuring six tenths of a mile wide and two miles long, rising to an elevation of 930-feet. This group of islands runs about four and a half miles from east to west, lying 14 miles off the coast of Ventura.

With no natural harbor, this island of sheer cliffs has no dock in which to land. The boat, backed up against the rocks, is held by the running motor, allowing passengers to disembark and scurry up the scaffolding mounted into the cliffs on the eastern side of the island. This short workout pays off when the top of the island is reached and the spectacular view unfolds. Anyone with an adventurous spirit and a love of remote places is sure to enjoy a day trip to Anacapa. The truly adventurous can plan to stay overnight in one of the seven campsites on the island. Each campsite is comprised of a picnic table, and storage box to secure food and trash from the mice and gulls that inhabit the island. There is no shade on the island except that generated by the buildings and outhouse-style rest room located adjacent to the campsites. There is no water on the island, so visitors must bring all the water and food needed to last their entire visit. Anything packed in, must be packed out, including all trash generated.

Anacapa Island was first discovered by Cabrillo in 1542. Captain George Vancouver named the island Anacapa in 1793. "Anacapa," comes from the Canalino Indian name "Enecapah" meaning "ever changing." Anacapa would eventually become the location for the last lighthouse built in California by the government.

No one disputed the need of a light for the Santa Barbara Channel. The debate where the lighthouse would be located had gone on as early as 1857, when the U.S. Coastal Survey had recommended building a lighthouse at Point Hueneme. After the sinking of the *Winfield Scott* in 1854, Anacapa was examined and determined to be an unrealistic location to build a lighthouse because of its rugged and remote location. The Lighthouse Board petitioned for a light on Anacapa, but in March 1873, the money appropriated by congress, went toward a light at Point Hueneme instead.

As time passed, traffic increased and more shipping accidents took place. In 1912, a metal tower erected on the east end of the island had a light mounted on top, fueled by acetylene. Showing the inadequacy of the move, the *Liebre* ran aground directly below the light in 1921.

In 1929, construction of a lighthouse began, but the construction company hired was not sufficiently expert to do the job, so construction began again with a new contractor. A derrick constructed at 55-feet above sea level, complimented another derrick placed at the top of the cliff in transporting materials onto the island.

Lit in 1932, Anacapa finally had a lighthouse. A third order Fresnel lens rested in a black cupola atop a 39-foot tower. Scaffolding mounted into the sheer cliffs on the eastern side of the island held a cradle to house small visiting boats. The only way to access the island was to be plucked from the sea and hoisted by a crane onto the island. In 1930, a light-keeper died when he fell from the stations platform. In 1934, the *USS California* responded to a distress call from the island when a light-keeper's wife fell from the island. A boat from the battleship took the woman to shore, where she was treated and recovered.

The light was replaced with an aero beacon when the station was automated in 1962. Coast Guard Seaman Ralph E. Lewis expressed his thoughts when the automation of the tower was imminent; "I'll really miss the place. The peaceful atmosphere, fresh air and an ocean on all sides cannot help but change your style of living after nearly three years. I only hope I can adjust to civilization again."

Removed from the tower in June 1990, the Fresnel lens now resides in the islands museum. Steve James, who was the islands maintenance

Anacapa Light Station
Photo courtesy of The United States Lighthouse Society

mechanic at the time, took several months removing the black paint that had covered the brass and bronze castings of the lens. Paint on the fittings allowed the avoidance of routine maintenance required to polish the lens.

In spring, colorful flowers inhabit the island, including the tree sunflower, or *Coreopsis*, a plant found only on the Channel Islands and a few isolated areas on the mainland. Just off the southeast end of the island is home to a 40-foot high arch reaching out of the water, the trademark of Anacapa and the Channel Islands National Park.

The island has taken advantage of renewable energy sources to limit any outside impact. The Park Service operates a variety of solar power systems. The main photo voltaic array, reconfigured in 1987, has since reduced diesel consumption by 96 percent. Before 1992, diesel generators ran 24 hours a day to operate the lighthouse, a costly operation in such a remote location. The USCG reconfigured the lighthouse, implemented conservation measures, and converted the system to operate as a standalone photo voltaic solar system. A small solar array provides electricity to the visitor center and bunkhouse. A photo voltaic system used for charging communications equipment batteries, operating lights, and ventilation for the campground pit toilets, powers an underwater video program as well.

The annual biodiesel (a clean burning alternative fuel, produced from domestic, renewable resources) consumption is less than 275 gallons, making the island totally petroleum free. The park believes it is now feasible to operate exclusively on renewable resources.

East Anacapa Island is 163 acres in size and has no water resources; water must be brought in by tanker once a year. Low flush toilets installed in 1992 reduced the islands water demand by 65 percent, and reduced the load on the evapotranspiration waste treatment system.

Since 1995, the facility has been operating cost free and without damage to the environment.

SANTA BARBARA LIGHTHOUSE

An elementary school is located where the once popular Santa Barbara Lighthouse once stood. Children play in the field overlooking the ocean in this peaceful seaside spot. Below the school and across the street is the light tower that replaced the original lighthouse back in 1935; residing in the backyard of the Santa Barbara coast guard housing unit. The remaining light is not the glamorous structure its predecessor was but a functional metal tower and rotating beacon.

The all-metal tower is 24-feet tall, and about three-feet square, performing its duty consistently as it has for over 70 years. The tower sits on the bluff surrounded by ice plant that blooms bright yellow when in season; a children's playground and a charming gazebo sit nearby. On the other side of the housing unit is La Mesa Neighborhood Park where, from the bridge, the back of the tower is visible. The tower is also visible from the driveway. The complex is fenced, gated, and is not open to the public.

One of the first seven lighthouses built in California, Santa Barbara Lighthouse, built on Dibblee's Hill, used the same design as other early west coast lighthouses. Housing a fourth order Fresnel lens, Santa Barbara Lighthouse began life in 1856. Albert J. Williams was the first light-keeper and his wife Julia, the assistant light-keeper. The Williams had four sons and three daughters, all born in the lighthouse. The lighthouse was an attractive building built from brick and stucco with a circular stairway in the living room that led to the light. Rain gutters fed the cistern that stored the water supply for the station.

Julia prided herself in the care she gave to the grounds and gardens, which she always took care to keep beautifully manicured and maintained. After four years, Williams left the post. From 1860 to 1865, four different light-keepers came and went from the Santa Barbara Lighthouse. When asked to return to his former post, Albert Williams turned down the assignment, but his wife Julia accepted. For more than 40 years, she climbed the three flights of stairs every night and personally maintained the light. Julia was only out of sight of the lighthouse on two occasions, once for the birth of one of her sons, and once for the wedding of one of her sons. Julia was the second woman light-keeper in California; the first was Charlotte Layton, light-keeper of Point Pinos Lighthouse in Monterey.

Julia maintained the light beautifully, raised her children, and tended the gardens around the lighthouse, making the Santa Barbara Lighthouse somewhat of a showplace in town. Julia was a well-liked and respected member of the community and somewhat of a local celebrity, since the lighthouse was such a popular attraction to see at the time. When she retired she was the oldest incumbent light-keeper in California. During her service, she saw one of her children and her husband pass away at the

Santa Barbara Lighthouse
Photo courtesy of The United States Lighthouse Society

lighthouse and showed unwavering dedication to her position. In 1905 at the age of 79, Julia fell and broke her hip. No longer able to tend the light, she found herself in Santa Barbara's "Cottage Hospital" bedridden for six years from injuries sustained while in the performance of her duty. President Theodore Roosevelt visited Julia in 1908, and just three years later, Julia F. Williams, one of California's great light-keepers passed away at the age of 85.

After serving at Point Conception, Harley Weeks became the light-keeper of Santa Barbara light. After his death, his wife became light-keeper and finally his son.

A large earthquake shook the Santa Barbara region at 6:45 a.m., on June 29, 1925, damaging the lighthouse beyond repair; those inside escaped with only minor injuries. The Lighthouse was a complete loss, and its demolition along with all of the surrounding buildings was deemed necessary. A temporary light stood until 1935, when the structure used today began life. The lamp used from 1925 until 1977, is on display at Point Vicente.

POINT CONCEPTION

What an awesome feeling of isolation the families stationed here must have felt. Entering the lighthouse is like stepping back in time. So remote is this lighthouse that it has escaped the reach of thieves and vandals; Point Conception maintains its integrity. This is the only lighthouse in California with the original weights used to drive the clockworks still intact. Even the diamond shaped reflectors placed in the floor of the lantern room all remain. A remarkable and beautiful structure, Point Conception has a design unique in California; the front rooms have beautiful wooden paneled walls and cabinets shipped from Russia. The level on which the lighthouse resides has only one remaining structure, the oil house, a small empty concrete building. All that remains on the cliff above, is a single dwelling erected in the 1960s.

Standing majestically on the rocky coast, north of the Santa Barbara Channel, Point Conception marks the southern extremity of one of the most hazardous coasts in the world, where rough seas are common. Known as the "Cape Horn of the Pacific," this southern California point is the corner of the state where the coast changes directions from east to west to north to south. Swift currents, strong winds, and sudden weather changes create dramatic marine and terrestrial ecosystems and add a greater degree of danger for seamen.

After construction on Point Conception began, the Lighthouse Board called for all of California's lighthouses to be equipped with Fresnel lenses. The tower, originally designed for an Argand oil lamp was too small to support the new first order lens ordered from France. When Major Hartman Bache, the pacific coast lighthouse inspector, found that the lens would not fit into the constructed tower, he refused to pay the builders until a new tower, set back from the lighthouse with the diameter increased to accommodate the lighting apparatus, rose in its place.

An entire year passed before the lamp and lens arrived after George Parkinson, the first light-keeper, began his tenure. Parkinson expressed his opinion about his position to Bache in a letter, complaining about the remoteness of his station, the cost of supplies, and the lack of pay. Parkinson felt the location was a "dreadful promontory of desolation." The Village of Santa Barbara, 65 miles away, was the nearest community, and the post office had not heard of Point Conception, so it took three months to deliver the reply.

Between Point Arguello and Point Conception the waters are scattered with the remains of numerous ships. While waiting for the Fresnel lens to arrive from France, the steamer *Yankee Blade* went aground on the rocks between Point Arguello and Point Conception, while traveling at full speed in a dense fog. The ship, designed with a 22-inch oak hull to withstand the harshest of weather, provided luxurious accommodations. The ships manifest showed only 819 people, but the ship was actually carrying as many as 1,200 passengers, including 125 crew members, and stowaways attempting to escape justice. At the very least, $153,000 in gold dust and nuggets were being stored on board.

During the gold rush, the man who could boast having the fastest ship, booked more passengers. San Francisco to Panama was the regular route for the *Yankee Blade,* and its pilot Captain Randall wanted to have the fastest ship covering the route. Unfortunately, on his first two trips, an over-eager Randall had made errors that had cost him the lead. Randall had only managed to beat his competitor once because the other ship had been detained for four hours. Before the third trip of the new vessel began, an advertisement appeared in the *Daily Alta California*: a $5,000 wager that the *Yankee Blade* would steam into Panama on its trip from San Francisco before the *Sonora.* The person offering the wager remained anonymous, but speculation was that Captain Randall was behind the challenge.

When the *Yankee Blade* left the San Francisco Bay, Captain Randall immediately began to hug the shore, while the *Sonora* sailed further out to sea before making its turn south. Staying dangerously close to shore, while traveling in heavy fog, Captain Randall, nevertheless kept the ship at full speed, in hopes of shaving time off his passage. The Captain was in the saloon having drinks with one of the passengers when suddenly the ship heaved forward in the water. Glasses flew from the bar; the sound of splitting timbers filled the air, and passengers were thrown to the ground. The great oak hull cracked, as the ship struck with full force into the rocks off Point Arguello, tearing a 12-foot long gash in the hull below the waterline.

Captain Randall knew at once the ship was lost. He and some of the crew took a small boat and searched for a safe place to land. Captain Randall left his teenage son Henry Randall Jr. in charge, but young Henry was thoroughly incapable of handling the ship during the disaster.

Jim Turner, a notorious San Francisco criminal indicted for assault with a deadly weapon, had stowed away on the *Yankee Blade* with his gang in hopes of escape and was now terrorizing the passengers. Some of the remaining crew joined with Turner and his men and broke into the ships liquor stores. Turner now took advantage of the passengers by relieving them of any extra weight they may be carrying in the form of gold or other valuables. Turner and his gang tried to commandeer the remaining boats for themselves, but male passengers drew their guns on the gang and allowed the women and children to get into the boats. Some of Turner's men managed to seize one boat and filled it with gold and loot, but in their

Point Conception Light Station
Photo courtesy of The United States Lighthouse Society

attempt to escape the boat sunk, and the criminals got dragged down by the weight of their ill-gotten gain. The ship was within 200-yards of the shore when it went down, and 415 perished in the wreck. All of the gold went to the bottom of the ocean, and Jim Turner escaped. In the end, Captain Henry Randall, the individual responsible for the sinking of the *Yankee Blade* became a wealthy man. Randall headed the salvage company that pinpointed the exact location of the *Yankee Blade* and recovered the gold that went down with the ship.

Point Conception's new light and lens finally made their debut in February 1856, in a 52-foot tower. In January 1857, the massive Fort Tejon earthquake hit the southern California region, causing major damage to the dwelling surrounding the tower. This event was a large contributor to what would eventually undermine the original lighthouse structure causing its replacement 25 years later.

In 1872, a steam whistle installed at Point Conception on the bluff 100-feet below the lighthouse began warning ships in place of the fog bell, which was moved to Yerba Buena Island where it was put into service two years later.

The Lighthouse Board reported in 1875, that the station was in poor condition and needed replacement because the structure had settled, and cracks had developed. Although denied, five years later the report to congress stated that the tower needed reinforcement with wooden supports to help hold up the tower. So the following year appropriations were made to build a new dwelling and tower. A fourth order lens went into operation, installed on a platform erected on the old tower, while the first order lens made its move to the new tower.

On June 20, 1883, the second incarnation of the lighthouse began its operation at Point Conception, now located on the bluff 115-feet below the cliff on which it had previously resided. The Lighthouse Board decided that the elevation of the original light was too high, thus being obscured during periods of heavy fog, so the lighthouse moved closer to the water so it could be easily seen from the sea. The entire interior of the original tower was migrated to the new lighthouse. After relocating the contents, crews removed the original tower to just below the roof line of the structure, then sealed up the opening and made extensive repairs to that side of the dwelling. This residence continued operation until 1906, when a replacement duplex structure at the top of the cliff was completed. An additional dwelling built in 1912, made way for the removal of the original lighthouse. The complex now consisted of the lighthouse, four keepers' dwellings, a barn, a washhouse, a bunkhouse, a carpenter shop, a storehouse and an oil house. A long wooden staircase went from the dwellings above down to a cement walkway on the lighthouse level. Three different cisterns were fed from a nearby spring that supplied water to the station. Electricity did not come to the point until 1948, somewhat later than most lighthouses.

When automation reached the lighthouse in 1973, an electric motor replaced the original mechanism used to rotate the lens (a 150 pound weight descending from a clockwork device that provided the power to turn the light). The first order Fresnel lens continued to operate until 1999, when switching to a modern beacon outweighed the cost of maintaining the massive first order lens, which remains in the cupola of this magnificent edifice. Not visible from any beach, there is no way to visit Point Conception; it is only visible from the sea.

Point Arguello

Situated on the outer shore of an outcropping of land called Point Arguello, named in honor of Jose Mario Arguello, the original lighthouse began its operation in February 1901. Point Arguello was fitted with the fourth order Fresnel lens originally used in the Point Hueneme Lighthouse. The building used a blueprint somewhat similar to the lighthouse at Point Cabrillo, built eight years later. The tower stood at the western end of a single story fog signal building that was outfitted with a compressed air fog signal. The dwellings were located a short distance up a dirt road to the east.

Unfortunately, the lighthouse did not quell the shipwrecks in the area. On a warm July morning in 1911, the steamer *Santa Rosa* ran aground on the rocks just north of the light station. With the ship lying perpendicular to the beach, an attempt at a rescue proved futile when two steamers came to the aid of the ailing ship. A cable strung between the two healthy steamers, attached to the stranded ship only managed to face it out to sea, creating tension on the cable so great that it snapped, allowing the vessel to swing back into the rocks breaking her in two. Light-keeper W. A. Henderson attempted to assist the victims by shuttling the passengers to safety in a lifeboat, but the surf was too dangerous. People on shore waded into the surf and created a human chain to pull people out of the surf. Suspended between the ship and the nearby train trestle, a life buoy with a suspended canvas sling helped in pulling passengers from the vessel to the beach. Light-keeper Henderson, after spending the entire day rescuing passengers, was back to the lighthouse by 11:30 that night, cold, tired, hungry, and wet.

Erosion had taken its toll against the outcropping of land the tower rested on, and in 1911, a separate tower built along side of the fog signal building took the place of the original lighthouse. The tower was razed in 1934, when a skeleton tower was erected housing a pair of revolving aero beacons.

The Navy's greatest navigational tragedy took place off the coast of Point Arguello in September of 1923. Destroyer Squadron Eleven left San Francisco Bay at 7:30 a.m., for a morning of combat maneuvers, followed by a 20-knot run south, and a night passage through the Santa Barbara Channel. That afternoon the 14 destroyers created a column formation led by their flagship, the USS *Delphy*. As the day progressed, the squadron was enveloped in a heavy fog.

At 9 p.m., off an isolated coastal headland, locally known as Honda Point, officially called Point Pedernales, the squadron commander Captain Edward H. Watson and two other experienced navigators on board *Delphy* used dead reckoning to maneuver the ship. Dead Reckoning is a method in

Point Arguello Light Station
Photo courtesy of The United States Lighthouse Society

which you take the course and distance from your origin to your destination, determine your speed, and how long you have been traveling, and that, (in theory) will give you the current location at the time of your reckoning.

The new radio direction finding (RDF) station at Point Arguello, a few miles south of Honda, reported to the squadron that it was still to the north. The Captain and his navigators did not completely trust the new RDF system and believing the squadron had already passed Point Arguello, discounted this information. Using the bearings obtained from their calculations, Destroyer Squadron Eleven was ordered to turn eastward, with each ship following the *Delphy*.

In reality, the Squadron was several miles north and further east than *Delphy's* navigators believed. About five minutes after making her turn, the *Delphy* slammed into the Honda shore. Just a few hundred yards astern, the USS *S. P. Lee* saw the *Delphy* suddenly stop, and sharply turned to port, and in doing so, she struck the hidden coast to the north of *Delphy*. Right behind, the USS *Young* had no time to turn before ripping open her hull on the submerged rocks and turning onto her starboard side. The *Woodbury* and *Nicholas*, the next two destroyers in line, turned right and left respectively, but could not avoid the rocks. The USS *Farragut* backed away with relatively minor damage, and the USS *Fuller* piled up near the

Woodbury. The *Somers,* and USS *Percival* both escaped the disaster, but the USS *Chauncey* while attempting to rescue the men of the capsized USS *Young* went aground as well. The *Kennedy, Paul Hamilton, Stoddert,* and *Thompson,* the last four destroyers in the formation, steered clear of the coast and were unharmed. Hundreds of crew members suddenly found themselves fighting for survival in total darkness and in freezing water, struggling against waves that were crashing against the rocky shore. Amazingly, there were only 23 lives lost in the wreckage. Captain Watson vigorously organized rescues and took survival measures for the several hundred shipwrecked sailors. Watson took full responsibility for the decisions he made that led to the tragedy. Watson was court marshaled, and could rise no higher in the Navy ranks. Point Arguello light-keepers Gotford Olson, Arvel Settles, and Jesse Mygrants received Navy commendations for the rescuing efforts they made to save the shipwrecked troops during the disaster.

The Coast Guard removed the original dwellings in 1967. All that remains of the light at Point Arguello is a small platform that rests atop a post, consisting of a small rotating optic, a backup beacon, and foghorn. The site is now part of Vandenberg Air Force Base and is off limits to the public but is visible from Amtrak trains that pass.

SAN LUIS OBISPO

San Luis Obispo Light Station
Photo courtesy of The United States Lighthouse Society

Reservations are required to access the lighthouse at Port San Luis, and to attend a free docent led hike along the Pecho trail. Visitors are given the grand tour of this isolated lighthouse and the surrounding property. The three and a half mile hike winds along the San Luis Headland to the light station. Hikers meet at the trail head just outside the gates of the Point Diablo nuclear facility on Avila beach. The hike takes about an hour to reach the destination, and along the way the docents regale visitors with local history.

Restoration is ongoing at this largely intact station. Most of the outside work is complete, and the meticulous recreation continues on the interior. The Lighthouse, located on the southwestern end of the headland, is only visible from the water. Volunteers have removed the non-native ice plant, allowing the area to bloom once again with its native Periwinkle Vinca major.

Recommendations to build a lighthouse for the port of San Luis (originally known as Port Harford) started as early as the 1860s. By the early 1870s, traffic at the port had increased to an average of one ship arriving each day, making the need for a lighthouse obvious to the citizens of San Luis Obispo County. It was the most important port south of San Francisco, and business was increasing yearly.

In May 1888, the *Queen of the Pacific* started to take on water about 2:00 a.m., approximately 15 miles from Port Harford. The captain was able to turn the ship and slowly bring it toward the port. Within 500-feet of the pier, the steamship sank to the bottom in just 22-feet of water; no lives were lost in the accident, but this incident pushed forward plans for a lighthouse at Port Harford.

Good weather prevailed eight or nine months out of the year, and during the other months weather at the port was never really that bad. The light would perform not only as a primary coast light but as a guide to Port Harford as well. With commerce came more people, increasing the number of passenger ships that plied the west coast waters. For protection, the shipping company maintained a private light for vessels entering the port. The company even considered building a fog-signal at their own expense.

By executive reservation, the Lighthouse Board acquired Whalers Island, located about 500-feet from San Luis Head, with the option to purchase another 30 acres on the Headland. If need be, the Board was prepared to place either the light or the fog signal on the Head and locate the other on the adjacent Island.

San Luis Head or Whalers Rock is midway between Point Conception and Piedras Blancas, a distance of 94 miles. On June 30, 1890, the Victorian style lighthouse first began its operation. The lamp, fueled by whale oil, (later kerosene and finally, electricity) provided the light source for the fourth order Fresnel lens. A system of heavy weights driven by a clockwork mechanism turned the lens, and had to be wound every 12 hours. The wharf, an integral aspect of the station, provided a landing for supplies, which came by way of steamer.

In 1894, San Luis Obispo welcomed the new railroad that terminated at Port Harford. Now lumber and other products that moved by ship could be off-loaded directly onto railcars.

On the lighthouse reservation, an area was cleared and cemented for a water-shed that would feed the under-ground cisterns which had a capacity of 100,000 gallons of water. After its completion, the rainfall accumulation was not significant enough to support the operation of the fog-signal, so a pipe line was laid from Pacho Creek, about three and a half miles away, which provided an unlimited supply of good water. Electric light replaced the old kerosene lamp in the tower in 1933, and a modern wood frame duplex, built in 1961, replaced the original assistant light-keeper's home, which was simply pushed over the cliff. The original Fresnel lens was replaced with a modern electric beacon in 1969, which stayed in use until the station closed in 1974. An automatic fog detector switches the light and horns on when coastal fog drifts within four miles of San Luis Head.

PIEDRAS BLANCAS

On his exploration of the coast of California in the year 1542, Juan Rodriguez Cabrillo became the first man to record sighting the gleaming white rocks of Piedras Blancas, north of San Simeon Bay. Between Point Pinos to the north and Point Conception to the south is a distance of 150 miles. The dangerous rocks surrounding the point at Piedras Blancas were the impetus for choosing it as a perfect location to build a lighthouse station. In June 1872, congress approved appropriations for a first order light at Piedras Blancas.

Located on the north entrance to San Simeon Bay, three miles from Hearst Castle, Piedras Blancas has the appearance more like a tower out of medieval times. Three white rocks that sit just off the point are responsible for the unique name Piedras Blancas, meaning "white rocks". San Simeon Bay, just south of the point, was the perfect safe harbor for small trading schooners and brigs when the northwest wind would begin to blow.

When completed the tower had a double wall of brick separated by airspace, creating a wall four-feet-ten-inches thick at the base. The walls taper to a thickness of 18-inches at the top; this method of construction kept the structure from deteriorating in the moist sea air.

Piedras Blancas Light Station
Photo courtesy of The United States Lighthouse Society

Four shanties rose for the laborers and mechanics to live in during construction. Work on the fog signal ceased after the completion of the tower, while the keepers' dwelling was completed. During this time, the keepers lived in the same shanties that had provided for the workers. Since the shanties would not provide adequate shelter during the rainy season, the dwellings had to take precedence over the fog signal. After the keepers' dwelling, sometimes referred to as the triplex was completed, one of the shanties would be used as a chicken house and the others would have many uses until being demolished around 1960.

The 12-room Victorian two-story triplex with three baths and an attic was completed before the rains came in the winter of 1875. Located 125-feet northeast of the tower, the triplex housed all three keepers and their families. The station consisted of the tower, the triplex, a barn, four chicken coops, and two oil houses. Eight redwood tanks with a sum total capacity of 125,000 gallons held the water necessary for the station.

Lit for the first time on February 15, 1875, the lamp used five concentric wicks burning lard oil. Light-keepers had the hourly task of winding the clockwork mechanism that kept the lens rotating smoothly on its chariot wheels. Heavy weights pulled on the great device to turn the multi-ton first order Fresnel lens.

In early 1876, Captain Lorin Vincent Thorndyke took the post of head keeper, serving in that capacity until he retired in 1906 at the age of 75. Mrs. Thorndyke died when her youngest son, Emory, was four years old. The Captain was left with the responsibility of raising his sons, Lorin V. and Emory, both of whom had been born at the lighthouse. Thorndyke would work the early evening shift from 6 p.m., to 10 p.m., giving him the opportunity to be home all through the night with his family. The remaining two shifts alternated between the remaining two assistant keepers

For years, the Lighthouse Board had petitioned Congress to build a fog signal on Point Buchon, which lays about 17 miles from San Luis Obispo, but no funds had been forthcoming. In 1902, the board recommended to the Senate Committee on Commerce that they build the fog signal at Piedras Blancas instead. In September 1903, John Emory Thorndyke, the son of Captain Lorin V. Thorndyke, became the first individual hired as a third assistant keeper for Piedras Blancas.

In 1949, a major storm broke the windows of the lantern house, prompting the removal of the cupola and the replacement of the Fresnel lens with an aero-beacon. The Cambria Lions Club helped save the first order Fresnel from destruction in 1951, putting it on display outside the Veterans Building downtown. In 1990 after 39 years of erosion and wear, restoration of the lens and lantern house led to its new placement on display

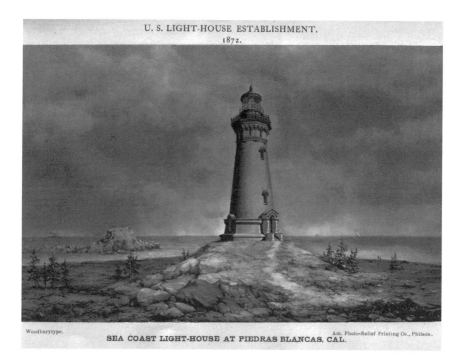

U. S. LIGHT-HOUSE ESTABLISHMENT.
1872.

Woodburytype.   Am. Photo-Relief Printing Co., Philada.
SEA COAST LIGHT-HOUSE AT PIEDRAS BLANCAS, CAL.

Piedras Blancas Light Station
Image courtesy of The Bureau of Land Management

at the Pinedorado Grounds in Cambria.

Sold in 1960 for the token sum of one dollar, the quarters built in 1906, moved to Chatham Street in Cambria. After remodeling and restoration by Cambria contractor Sandy Dustman, the home became a vacation rental. The rest of the quarters were razed in 1960, making room for four new modern Coast Guard residences. The station was automated in 1975.

Piedras Blancas Light House has become the home of the Western Ecological Research Center, part of the U.S. Geological Survey, responsible for many types of research.

In 2001, possession of Piedras Blancas transferred to the Bureau of Land Management (BLM), which officially took control of the lighthouse as a private aid to navigation, and laid the groundwork for a stabilization and restoration project. Volunteers have begun a beautification process of removing weeds and encouraging the growth of native plants. Piedras Blancas Lighthouse is open for limited public tours led by interpretive specialists from BLM, Hearst Castle, or the light station's volunteer corps.

POINT SUR

Poised 36 stories above the ocean on the edge of a large volcanic rock, sits Point Sur, California's most complete light station. Kept in continuous operation since 1889, the lighthouse is now part of California State Parks. Point Sur docents lead walking tours telling stories of the adventurous souls that lived at the station, and recounting interesting tales of the disasters and rescues associated with this unique light station.

Instrumental in the restoration of Point Sur Light Station has been the Central Coast Lighthouse Keepers. The group is a membership-based, non-profit corporation dedicated to preserving the maritime heritage of the central coast of California, especially the aids to navigation.

Named "Punta que aparece como isla" or "Point which appears as an island," by Sebastian Vizcaino in 1603, Point Sur can be surrounded by water during fierce storms effectively turning the huge rock into an island. The wreck of the *Ventura* in April 1875 highlighted the need for a lighthouse on Point Sur. A cargo steamer, the *Ventura*, was on its way from San Francisco to Anaheim with 186 people onboard. Captain George Fake was reportedly drunk when the *Ventura* struck an outcropping of rocks obscured by thick fog two miles north of Point Sur.

Delays put off construction until 1887, when the light station at Point Sur began to rise. Point Sur could supply no water, so the supply came from a well located in the sand flats at the base of the rock. To build a lighthouse on Point Sur would be a formidable task, and to begin, high explosives blasted away the top 80-feet of the rock to accommodate the light station. Workers constructed a road that stretched between the mainland and Point Sur. Also built was a 395-step stairway to the top of the rock. Running alongside the stairs was track for a railway that climbed up the face of Point Sur. A steam donkey engine was used to hoist supplies up to the station from 1887-1900, when a road was finally built.

Point Sur Light Station beamed its light out over the Pacific for the first time on August 1, 1889. Perched on top of the rock sits the light-keepers' house, assistant light-keeper house or triplex, the water tower, a blacksmith shop, barn, garage, cistern, and pump house. Boilers, using wood as fuel, burned an average of 100 cords of redwood and oak annually to create the steam needed for the fog signal whistles to produce their piercing wail.

Life on Point Sur was an isolated existence for a light-keeper and his family. The trip to the bustling seaport of Monterey was a full day's journey on a dangerous trail, so trips were infrequent. The light station had to be self-sufficient. The four families living on the rock planted vegetable gardens and raised livestock. The light-keepers handled all construction and repair jobs as part of their daily duties.

Every four months a tender loaded with provisions would anchor south of the station. A skiff would land on the windswept beach, and supplies were hoisted to the top by the steam donkey engine or taken by mule-drawn wagons.

The seclusion of the station created a problem in educating the light-keeper's children. The children would stay with family friends during the week, while attending school on the mainland, and spent the weekends on the rock. Head light-keeper William Mollering petitioned Monterey County in 1927 for a school for the children of Point Sur. Schools required a minimum of six students, only five children of school age resided at the station, so young Billy Mollering had his age advanced on paper. A one-room schoolhouse soon rose on the nearby sand flats

Light-keeper Thomas Henderson witnessed the helium-filled *USS Macon,* the largest aircraft the world had ever seen, crash offshore from Point Sur. An aluminum-framed dirigible, twice the width of the *Titanic*

Point Sur School, 1950
Photo courtesy of The United States Lighthouse Society

Point Sur Light Station
Photo courtesy of The United States Lighthouse Society

and three times longer than a 747, belonged to the Navy's "lighter-than-air" aviation program. The *Macon* suddenly found itself in a rainstorm off Point Sur when a large gust of wind broke the upper tail fin, which tore holes in some of its helium cells causing the huge airship to lose altitude. Miraculously all but two of its 83 crew managed to escape.

State Highway One completed in 1937, runs within one mile of the rock, and over time has managed to make the lighthouse seem a little less isolated. In the 1970s, automation of the light allowed the removal of the last of the Coast Guard personnel from the station. Regular visits from the Coast Guard keep the equipment in first-rate order. Tourists now have the opportunity to explore this once remote lighthouse. The original first order lens from Point Sur resides at the Stanton Maritime Museum in Monterey.

POINT PINOS

Surrounded by the Pacific Grove Golf Course, a quarter of a mile from the sea, Point Pinos lighthouse, the oldest continuous operating lighthouse on the west coast, sits among the wind bent cypress trees.

Punta de los Pinos or Point of the Pines was named by Sebastian Vizcaino in 1602, when pines covered the area, almost reaching the water's edge. Jutting out from the southern entrance to Monterey Bay, Point Pinos offered a significant hazard to mariners, and with the discovery of gold in California, shipping along the coast increased dramatically.

With an eye toward constructing a new lighthouse, the government purchased 25 acres of the Rancho Punta de los Pinos. The barkentine sailing ship *Oriole* sailed from San Francisco in March of 1853, carrying the men and materials necessary for the building of Point Pinos.

Granite, quarried on site, was the material used to build the lighthouse and the surrounding buildings. The house had wood plank floors, and a brick tower with an iron and brass lantern room. Point Pinos was scheduled to receive a second order lens from France, but there were continual delays. A third order Fresnel lens originally planned for the Battery Point Lighthouse in San Francisco (later known as Fort Point) found its home at Point Pinos instead. Battery Point Lighthouse, built using the same design as Point Pinos, had seen its premature demise to make way for the new Army Fort, leaving the lens unused until February 1, 1855, when Point Pinos shone the light for the first time.

Forced up to the lamp by a gravity-operated piston, sperm whale oil, stored in a tank below, saturated the wick used to illuminate the lamp. Point Pinos was the only California lighthouse to have used sperm whale oil which was replaced with lard oil sometime in the 1860s, then kerosene, and ultimately electricity.

After serving in the U.S. Army artillery regiment as a sergeant, Charles Layton came to California during the mad rush of 1849, seeking his fortune in the gold fields. When Layton moved on, he settled in Monterey and became the appointed light-keeper of the Point Pinos Lighthouse in September 1854. Layton remained light-keeper until an unfortunate run-in with a notorious outlaw robbed him of his job and life. In early November of 1855, Anastasio Garcia, an outlaw wanted for the murder of two men, was on the run from the law. Sheriff Keating gathered a posse of men including Charles Layton, to ride with him to Salinas to capture Garcia. When they arrived at the house where Garcia holed up, Layton and two others took the back of the house, and the rest of the men took the front. Garcia came out the back and opened fire upon the men, killing Joaquin de la Torra and seriously injuring Mr. Beckwith, who would later die from his wounds. Charles Layton, hit with a pistol ball, had the first joint on his index finger and a second finger at the knuckle blown off. The ball then hit his pistol, ricocheted off and lodged in his stomach. Layton, bleeding profusely, managed to make his way six miles. He was discovered and brought to the Washington hotel, and died on November 19, 1855-the fourth victim of Anastasio Garcia in one week.

Charles Layton left a wife, Charlotte, four small children, and a community that loved and respected the man who had selflessly given 16 years of his life to the service of his country. Garcia fled to Los Angeles and authorities swiftly apprehended and returned him to Monterey, where a group of vigilantes broke into the jail and hung him. Monterey in the 1800s was still a wild untamed frontier that saw over 60 murders during the three-year period between 1853 and 1856. Not only did animals like Garcia roam the territory, but wild animals as well. Mountain lions, deer, and grizzly bears were regular inhabitants of the area around the lighthouse.

When Charles Layton died, a group of concerned Monterey citizens gathered a petition requesting the appointment of his wife Charlotte as light-keeper of Point Pinos. Charlotte would be the first woman light-keeper in the state, beginning in January 1856. When she married her assistant light-keeper George Harris in August 1860, he replaced her as

Point Pinos Lighthouse
Photo courtesy of The United States Lighthouse Society

the primary light-keeper.

Appointed light-keeper in 1871, Allen L. Luce would see great changes take place during his tenure as Monterey and Pacific Grove grew. It was while Luce was keeper, that many improvements were made, which included water making its way through a pump to the lighthouse, the coming of the railroad, the development of Pacific Grove, and the increase of tourism.

In 1879, a tall thin Scottish man visited the lighthouse. Luce made him feel at home and gave the young man the grand tour, treating him with his usual hospitality. The writer was Robert Louis Stevenson, who would go on to pen The Strange Case of Dr. Jekyll and Mr. Hyde, Treasure Island and Kidnapped as well as many others. Stevenson was captivated by the beauty of the area, but he was also impressed with the immaculate lighthouse. Luce won over Stevenson with his many artistic endeavors, such as his model ships, oil paintings, piano playing abilities and his courteous hospitality. So much so that Stevenson included seven lines of description about Luce in his next essay entitled,

"The Old Pacific Capitol"
"Westward is Point Pinos, with the
lighthouse in a wilderness of sand, where
you will find the light-keeper playing
the piano, making models and bows and
arrows, studying dawn and sunrise in
amateur oil-painting, and with a dozen
other elegant pursuits and interests to
surprise his brave, old-country rivals."

It is not at all surprising that Stevenson had an interest in the lighthouse, as he came from a family of light-keepers. The Royal Scottish Society of Arts had bestowed the society's silver medal on his paper "On a New Form of Intermittent Light for Lighthouses" an explanation of the economical combination of revolving mirrors and oil-burning lamps, which was written during his student years.

The water supply for Point Pinos was collected by capturing runoff from the roof. Decorative lion's heads surrounding the cupola sent water spewing forth from their mouths onto the balcony when it rained, where it was redirected onto the roof below. Once caught in the eves, the water ran down pipes into the cistern below. During years with low rainfall, the water supply was short and other times the water was fouled and unfit for drinking. During these times, a supplemental supply, hauled from a distance, came at a premium expense. In 1885, water originating from the headwaters of the Carmel was directed to the lighthouse from the Pacific Improvement Company, who owned the hotel near Monterey.

Julia Fish had traveled to Shanghai, China, with her husband Dr. Melanchthon Fish, where he was to be the Inspector of Imperial Customs. In 1858, Julia's younger sister Emily, just 16 years old, traveled to Shanghai to visit her sister and her husband. After Julia died in childbirth, Emily, just 17, married Melancthon Fish and raised his daughter Juliet as her own. Years later, before Dr. Fish's death, his daughter Juliet married Lt. Commander Henry E. Nichols, the lighthouse inspector for the 12th district. When the position opened up for a lighthouse keeper at Point Pinos, Nichols arranged for Emily to take the job. After the death of Henry E. Nichols in 1898, during the Spanish American War, the Lighthouse Board appointed Juliet Nichols light-keeper of the Point Knox lighthouse on Angel Island in the San Francisco Bay.

On April 18, 1906, at about 5:13 a.m., the violent San Francisco earthquake struck the northern California coast. At Point Pinos, Emily Fish heard strange noises coming from the barn just before the quake struck; the horses were pounding the floor, and the cows were uneasy. When it hit, the quake enlarged a crack in the brick tower and bent the connecting tubes in the lens, loosening the prisms and rendering the lens unworkable. In the wood house, water sloshed out of the tank and covered the floor.

The lens and lantern, removed just following the quake for safety, allowed the reduction of the tower walls to about five-feet below the lantern floor. Using the same dimensions and design from the original tower, reinforced concrete replaced the one-foot thick brick masonry. Reinforced metal rods placed into newly drilled holes anchored the newly poured section to the existing wall. When completed, the light once again shone from the tower.

Emily Fish spent 21 years as the light-keeper at Point Pinos and was a well-respected member of the community. Emily Fish, 88 years old at her passing, had become a big part of California's lighthouse lore.

In 1915, following the departure of Emily Fish, power was run to the lighthouse from city service. Beginning in 1919, an electric light replaced the oil vapor lamp that had been in use since the turn of the century. After operating for 70 years exclusively as a lighthouse, an electric fog siren went into operation at the station in 1925.

Thomas Henderson's career as a lighthouse keeper began in 1925 when he answered a newspaper advertisement placed by the Department of Commerce. Henderson was first assigned to Point Arguello near Santa Barbara, then Pigeon Point, followed by Point Sur, where he was the officer in charge. Henderson witnessed the crash of the Navy dirigible *Macon* in 1936 off the Point Sur coast. His next assignment brought him to the post at Point Pinos where he stayed for 16 years. When Henderson retired, he received the Gallatin award for 30 years of public service.

During World War II, the light at Point Pinos went dark for the duration of the war. At 2:00 p.m., on December 20, 1941, just 13 days after the attack on Pearl Harbor, the Imperial Japanese Navy Submarine I-23 surfaced 20 miles from the southern tip of Monterey Bay off Cypress Point and fired eight or nine shells at the Richfield Oil Company tanker *Agwiworld.* Through quick evasive action, the *Agwiworld* managed to zigzag, avoiding the torpedoes, making it safely into the harbor about 4:00 p.m.

Beach patrols began and continued until late in 1944, the primary function was detecting and observing enemy vessels operating off the coast of California and transmitting the information to the Navy or Army command. In 1942, a battery of four 155mm Army coast defense guns from the 54th Coast Artillery at Fort Ord was placed in the sand dunes on the ocean side of Point Pinos Lighthouse. The Coast Guard built temporary redwood barracks units to the west of the lighthouse that housed 120 men for the Beach Patrol. Their trained dogs lived in kennels that were to the south near the horse stables.

In December 1967, negotiations between the Coast Guard and the city of Pacific Grove produced a lease of the lighthouse and surrounding property to the city of Pacific Grove with the intent of using the historical structure as a museum. The lighthouse, automated in 1975, had the radio beacon and fog signal deactivated in 1993 after the advent of GPS positioning. In 1995, the Adobe Chapter of the Questers, a non-profit organization, restored the parlor of the lighthouse to resemble the era when Emily Fish resided at the lighthouse.

SANTA CRUZ LIGHTHOUSE

Santa Cruz Lighthouse
Photo courtesy of The United States Lighthouse Society

The original Santa Cruz Lighthouse, torn down in 1948, shows no signs of ever having stood, but two other picturesque lights can be found in Santa Cruz. Neither of the structures is now nor have they ever been lighthouses; they are private aids to navigation and have never housed a light-keeper. The first is the Mark Abbott Memorial Lighthouse, which sits somewhat near where the original lighthouse was located and overlooks one of California's most famous surfing beaches. The small brick building housed the original lantern room and Fresnel lens from the Oakland Harbor lighthouse until 1996, when the lantern room was relocated to the Mobile Lighthouse in Alabama. The lighthouse, built in 1967, by the parents of Mark Abbott, a young surfer who drowned off the point, stands as a surfing museum and as a memorial to Mark, whose ashes reside under the tower.

Reports of huge pieces of earth breaking away due to erosion of the cliff have been going on since the original lighthouse resided on the bluff, and had to be relocated after just such an event. The memorial lighthouse continues to be in danger from the ongoing erosion, such as the major storm in 1983 that knocked 75-feet off the point.

The second light in Santa Cruz is Walton Light, located on the Santa Cruz breakwater across the bay from the Mark Abbott Memorial light.

Standing 42-feet in height, the tower replaced a harbor light that had been in use on the west jetty from 1964, to 1996. Built in memory of Derek Walton, a merchant seaman, the tower was dedicated on June 9, 2002. It was paid for with private donations, which included a generous contribution by his brother Charles Walton, a local sailor. The tower has a cylindrical inner core, which houses electrical equipment and a circular staircase of 42 steps leading to the top of the lighthouse. Trimmed in green and topped with a copper roofed lantern room, the walls of this white tower are four-feet-six-inches thick at the base.

Santa Cruz had been a major shipping port in the mid-nineteenth century but by the 1890s, shipping moved mostly through San Francisco, and Santa Cruz became a major tourist attraction instead.

Point Santa Cruz lies on the northern shore of Monterey Bay. The first attempt at building a lighthouse was made during the 1850s when funding was approved, but acquiring the land proved fruitless until 1868, when the property, then known as Phelan Park, was obtained. A small wooden structure with a tower first displayed its light from a fifth order lens on December 31, 1869. Ediz Hook Lighthouse in Washington State served as the model for this structure. The wicks in the lamp burned high quality lard oil, filtered from a half-gallon reservoir located up near the wick so that the heat would keep the oil fluid in cool weather. The type of fuel used changed to kerosene in 1870. Placed on rollers and moved 300-feet inland when threatened by erosion in 1878, the lighthouse was in an ongoing fight against Mother Nature's wrath. A fourth order lens installed in 1909 lasted until 1941, when an automated minor light nearby replaced the Santa Cruz Lighthouse.

In 1869, when he became the first light-keeper of the new Santa Cruz Lighthouse, Adna E. Hecox moved his wife, four sons, and his 15-year-old daughter Laura into the quaint little wooden house.

Born in Santa Cruz in January 1854, Laura had begun to take strolls along the beach collecting seashells, minerals, fossils, Indian artifacts, and unique items as therapy to help recuperate from a serious fall. Adna set up a room in the lighthouse for his daughter to display her treasures, which were greatly admired by everyone who visited. Many individuals would send artifacts of their own for her to add to her collection.

Laura had a deep interest in preserving and cataloging the various items she found as well as those sent from people all over the world. She made meticulous notations to document each piece and the location of the find. In an 1881 employment census, Laura registered her occupation as a "Conchologist" (a seashell expert) while the majority of the population registered as farm workers and homemakers. Laura Hecox had no such degree conferred upon her by a recognized educational institution but rather she conferred it upon herself. In her collection, she had items such as a skylight out of the deck of the schooner *Active* that ran ashore at Light House Point through no fault of the light-keeper. She was a member of many scientific societies and corresponded with many important naturalists of the time, including Professor A. G. Wetherby at the University of Cincinnati and Ralph Arnold a famous geologist and paleontologist.

Laura, who was mostly self-educated, did extensive research and cataloguing, contributing exhibits to the public library and the county fair, giving her the admiration of members from the scientific community. As thorough as her notes on mollusks and artifacts might have been, one thing they never were was personal. Her correspondence with others never included any information about herself, and her letters were strictly academic in tone.

Upon Adna Hecox's passing in 1883, Laura petitioned the Lighthouse Board for the position of light-keeper. Immediately installed into the position, Laura maintained the light much in the same meticulous manner as she had her collection. Quarterly inspections praised her for her orderly lighthouse, and attention to detail.

On weekends, Laura gave tours of the lighthouse to the public, giving them a chance to see not only the lighthouse but also the small one room museum she had created. Laura would even sweep off untidy visitors with a duster before she would allow them into the lighthouse.

In 1904, Andrew Carnegie donated $20,000 to build a new public library in Santa Cruz. The generosity of Carnegie inspired Laura Hecox, who made the decision to deed her collection to the new public library. The Hecox Museum, established in the basement of the building in 1905, displayed her collection of shells and fossils, impressive in its size and range. Laura never married, taking care of her elderly mother Margaret at the lighthouse until she passed on in 1908, at the age of 92. Laura Hecox never missed a day as keeper in the 34 years that she served. She retired in 1917 after living in the lighthouse for 48 years.

The last lighthouse keeper at Point Santa Cruz was Arthur Anderson who took over from Laura Hecox after her retirement. Anderson had been a lighthouse inspector and transferred from San Francisco to Santa Cruz as keeper, where he remained until the decommissioning of the lighthouse in 1941.

Two weeks after the bombing of Pearl Harbor, a Japanese submarine shelled an oil tanker 20 miles off the coast of Cypress Point in Monterey, followed by the shelling of an oil refinery in Santa Barbara in February. A real concern that a Japanese led mainland attack might occur prompted the Coast Guard to station the 54th Coast Artillery; an African-American unit, at Lighthouse Point. The segregated unit of black soldiers from North Carolina set up camps in Santa Cruz, Moss Landing, and Point Pinos. Some members of the community attempted to make parts of the city off-limits to the men of the 54th, but their Chaplain, Captain Baskerville, threatened to boycott the town. Race relations in Santa Cruz County changed forever, choosing economics over racism. Local churches and civic groups welcomed members with a series of dinners and local entertainment, with members of the unit always presenting themselves admirably. The 54th Battery was withdrawn from the area as the war wound down, leaving the town forever changed. Abandoned after the war, the lighthouse fell into disrepair leading to its demolition in 1948.

Walton Light

Photographs by
Kent Weymouth

Mark Abbott
Memorial Light

70

AÑO NUEVO ISLAND

Año Nuevo State Reserve is noteworthy for its most famous residents, elephant seals. They arrive in December or January and leave in early March. The greatest opportunity to observe the males among these huge beasts in mortal combat over the affection of their female counterparts is before the end of the year. By March and April, these enormous animals look as though they have lost a war, leaving the bodies of their brethren strewn along the beaches like a killing field. Fortunately, this is all just a game of fake out, as the elephant seals are very much alive, just looking unmistakably like Uncle Guido passed out on the couch after a big Thanksgiving Day meal. Elephant seals, for the purpose of diving for food, can hold their breath for up to 20 minutes, a practice they use on land as well, giving the impression to the casual viewer that they are no longer among the living. From time to time, a seal's flipper will come to life flinging warm sand over its body, letting you know it has not left this world, but simply has the patience for total lack of movement. The attraction of Año Nuevo is the elephant seal breeding, and not the lighthouse. You can see the island from the mainland, complete with original dwellings and the toppled tower. Unfortunately, those in search of lighthouse history will be disappointed, as the island is inaccessible and off limits to visitors.

In January 1603, Captain Sebastian Vizcaino, while mapping the pacific coast, charted a long tongue of land jutting out into the Pacific and named it "Punta Del Año Nuevo." Vizcaino made no note of the island that sits a short distance off shore, perhaps because 400 years ago this strip of land might have still been part of the mainland. In 1769, Miguel Costanso noted in his diary that a tongue of land extended from the beach west by north. Fray Juan Crespi while exploring the area from the beach, found evidence of Indian habitation but again made no note of an island.

A survey done by the State of California in 1857, and recorded in the *Book of Land Patents* shows a well-worn copy of the map in which the island is described as being connected to the mainland by a sandbar. Indicating that at this time in history, Año Nuevo Island was actually a peninsula. By 1869, this sand bar had apparently eroded away.

> "A point of land or small island on the Southwest extremity of said Rancho, surrounded by the waters of the Pacific Ocean at high tide which small island contains by estimation a few acres"

April 20, 1869, San Mateo Co., volume 9, page 226-7,
Deeds Indenture - between Loren Coburn and Rensselaer E. Steele

Año Nuevo Lighthouse
Photo courtesy of The United States Lighthouse Society

The ship *Coya* went aground on November 24, 1866, off Año Nuevo Island, also known at the time as Point New Years. The Captain's wife and child were among the 27 people who lost their lives. The final resting place for the 13 bodies recovered from the wreck, would be Franklin Point. According to *The Natural History of Año Nuevo* by *Burney Le Boeuf,* the coroner and Jury Report stated; "It seems to be very evident that it is the duty of the proper authorities to put a light on Point New Years."

Año Nuevo Island was sold to the U.S. Government along with the access rights in May 1870, along with Pigeon Point, six miles north (also part of the same Rancho).

A light-keepers' dwelling was constructed, and a steam fog-signal roared to life in May 1872, attracting local cows to the beach. It was not until 1890 that a light shone from a skeleton tower on Año Nuevo Island one half mile off shore.

Tragedy came to the island in April 1883, when light-keeper H. W. Colburn and assistant B. A. Ashley, two of the keepers of Año Nuevo along with two Pratt brothers, local ranchers who were visiting the light station, were lost at sea when rowing from the island to the mainland.

The steamer *Los Angeles* was passing the island around 4:00 p.m., when they heard the whistle blowing and noticed the hoisted flag hanging upside down, signifying a need for assistance. The steamer sent in a boat and Mrs. Colburn and Mrs. Ashley who had done their best to attract any passing vessels told the crew of the tragedy. A coastal search turned up no trace of the victims or the boat.

Pigeon Point first assistant light-keeper, J.C. Ryan was sent to Año Nuevo to assume charge of the station. After procuring a laborer to replace him as assistant at Pigeon Point, J.C. Ryan waited for the opportunity to cross to the island, restoring the light less than 48 hours after the tragedy. J.C. Ryan was promoted to head light-keeper, and chose for his assistant, John J. Galvin. Galvin just one day later on his return to the island from the mainland had his boat upset when a sudden gale arose, pitching one of his oars overboard. He safely returned to the mainland, where he spent the night, leaving Ryan alone with the evening watch.

Men arrived in May of 1886, to commence work on a sea wall to protect against erosion. They constructed a concrete wall 70-feet long with a height averaging 23-feet. The wall was as thick as 12-feet in some areas and never thinner than six-inches. A 14-foot long cave measuring two-feet high by two-feet wide, was located under the sandstone on the northern side of the island and filled with 176 barrels of concrete. A skeleton tower constructed on Año Nuevo in 1890, had the lens lantern mounted above a water tank.

The two light-keepers and their families were forced to share the small 1,000 square foot dwelling, by partitioning it in two. In 1906, after four years of requests for a second dwelling, a nine-room residence that included an indoor bathroom was constructed.

Four earthquakes took place in 1926; the first shock threw the original lamp to the floor, shattering it beyond repair. Replaced quickly with a back up, the lamp was knocked to the ground again just a few hours later when a second shock caused the tower to sway, once again destroying the lamp.

Abandoned in May 1948, the Año Nuevo Light Station became a breeding ground for the sea lions and elephant seals that populate the island. For safety reasons, the Coast Guard knocked over the tower in 1976. The buildings still remain along with the Victorian keepers' dwelling as part of the Año Nuevo State Reserve. This is a protected area used by the University of California at Santa Cruz as a research facility.

Año Nuevo is one of the largest mainland breeding grounds for elephant seals found in the world. Walking tours take place during breeding season, which runs from December through March. These popular walks last about two and one half hours. Considered by some to be moderately strenuous, conducted rain or shine, this outdoor hike over rolling hills and through sand may include high winds, and cold temperatures.

Adult seals begin to arrive on the beaches by mid-December. Bulls weighing up to 5,000 pounds engage in battles for breeding access to the females. Births begin in December and reach a peak in late January. By early March, most adult seals will return to the sea. Hundreds of weaned pups remain behind in March and learn to swim in the tide pools.

Año Nuevo Lighthouse
Photo courtesy of The United States Lighthouse Society

PIGEON POINT LIGHT STATION

Pigeon Point Light Station
Photo courtesy of The United States Lighthouse Society

With a tower 115-feet tall, Pigeon Point stands with Point Arena and St. George Reef Lighthouse as one of the tallest towers in California. Long peaceful stretches of beach lie alongside this majestic edifice, perfect for a picnic, a walk, or just relaxation.

In late December of 2001, two large sections of the brick and iron cornice broke away from this historic tower. California State Parks and the USCG, declared the building unsafe, closing it until repairs can be made. A chain-link fence erected around the lighthouse is to assure public safety until such a time that it is no longer necessary.

The grounds and the dwellings of Pigeon Point are part of the Golden Gate Council of Hostelling International. Along with Point Montara to the north, Pigeon Point serves as a youth hostel. The hostel remains open to the public. Unfortunately, the tower remains closed at the time of this writing.

"Whale Point," the rocky promontory off Pescadero was a whaling station used to hunt grey whales as they passed on their migration from the Arctic to Baja California. The point was a frequent stop-over port for schooners between San Francisco and Moro Bay and was used as a general shipping point of all products in the region. The area around the point was dangerous and home to many shipwrecks.

In June 1853, 129 days out, the three-masted clipper ship *Carrier*

Pigeon, ran aground during a storm, while on the southern approach to the San Francisco Bay at "Punto de las Ballenas" (Point of the Wales). The ship was just 500-feet from shore when it went down. The *Carrier Pigeon* was scheduled to transport gold between San Francisco, New York and Boston; she had a long narrow hull and was built for speed. She left Boston on her maiden voyage carrying 1,300 tons of cargo in her hold. After making good time around Cape Horn, she was sighted sailing past Santa Cruz.

The *Carrier Pigeon* soon found itself blanketed in a heavy fog. Believing he had headed further out to sea, nearing the Farallon Islands Captain Azariah Doane turned his ship to the east in hope of seeing land. Shortly after his change in course, the ship was suddenly split in two on the jagged rocks. The Captain and crew survived, but the ship and her cargo were lost. Such a dramatic disaster prompted the name of "Punto de las Ballenas" to be changed to Pigeon Point.

Bound for San Francisco in a heavy fog, the British ship *Sir John Franklin* struck rocks off the point in January 1865, destroying the ship, killing the Captain and 11 crew members. Six of the bodies were recovered, four seamen and two officers. Franklin Point is the resting place of the crew, and the officers were laid to rest in San Francisco, another case for building a lighthouse on Pigeon Point.

Pigeon Point Light Station - 1928
Photo courtesy of The United States Lighthouse Society

On September 10, 1871, the steam whistle at Pigeon Point went into operation, 14 months before the first order lens shone for the first time. One of only a handful of California lighthouses equipped with a first order Fresnel lens, the tower has the distinction of having received its lens from North Carolina's Cape Hatteras Lighthouse. The light first went into operation on November 15, 1872.

The *Columbia,* while sailing past Pigeon Point in July 1896, mistook the fog signal for a ships horn and in attempting to avoid a collision, steered directly into the rocks of Pigeon Point.

Automated in 1974, this proud tower stood alone, unmanned until September of 1977, when Albert Sandy Tucker was reassigned from the buoy tender *Black Hawthorne* to Pigeon Point as light-keeper. Tucker, stationed out of Alameda, made the drive daily from his home in Santa Cruz, getting in the habit of stopping at the light station and doing light chores around the place. Tucker would forward notes to the Aids to Navigation Team to inform them of repairs he had made. One day while the ship was being inspected by Captain Joe Blackett, Tucker worked up the nerve to propose the idea of living at the light station. This would bring him closer to Alameda where he could keep an eye on the place and try to help keep up with some maintenance. In *An Oral History: Tucker-An Interview with the Last Pigeon Point Light-keeper,* Tucker states that Captain Blackett felt that assignment to the *Black Hawthorne* and the light station would be too much for one man to handle, so he suggested, "We'll see if we can make you a light-keeper." After several months, Sandy Tucker got his transfer to Pigeon Point, moving himself and his wife into the largest dwelling at the station.

In the late seventies, many of the light stations experienced ongoing problems with vandalism, and Pigeon Point was rife with brash, persistent vandals. Tucker tried many methods that went unsuccessful, including numerous warning signs, a Doberman Pinscher and of course, the local police, but to no avail. The final solution was Lester the pig. Tucker had driven Lester home on his lap when he was just a small little pig, but as pigs often do, he grew, to some 800 pounds. A huge charging pig welcomed any vandals arriving at Pigeon Point light station. Lester's greeting discouraged vandals, and gave Lester some fun and exercise, albeit with less than willing playmates. Pigeon Point Light Station is now one of California's State Parks, and part of the Peninsula Open Space Trust.

POINT MONTARA

Point Montara Light Station-Original Tower
Photo courtesy of The United States Lighthouse Society

Point Montara is one of California's State Parks, and in addition the grounds and dwellings are also part of the Golden Gate Council of Hostelling International. Along with Pigeon Point Light Station to the south, these two light stations serve as youth hostels, offering cozy rooms with breathtaking views at modest and affordable prices. Nestled into the shore, Montara is one of the more accessible lighthouses in the state.

In October 1872, the *Aculeo*; a British square-rigged sailing ship with a cargo of sheet iron, steel, wire, and coal, departed from Liverpool for San Francisco, and struck the rocks near Point Montara. For a week, the sea battered the ship, breaking it apart on the rocks; all 21 members of the crew survived the wreck.

Point Montara was considered to be one of the most important stations on the approach to the San Francisco Bay. Located midway between Pigeon Point and the Golden Gate, Point Montara began its life as a 12-inch steam whistle on March 1, 1875.

In November 1900, a red lens lantern was hung on a post 300-feet south-west of the signal house, becoming the first light shone at Point Montara. In 1912, a skeleton tower was erected on site housing a fourth order Fresnel lens. The lamp transitioned to electricity in 1919. A third light-keeper, added in 1924, required the building of a new keeper's dwelling at the station.

The tower erected in 1912, had been so disintegrated by the saltwater spray that it was impractical to attempt to keep it in repair. In 1923 in Wellfleet, Massachusetts, the Mayo's Beach Lighthouse was removed from service and stored as surplus property. Correspondence marked as *letter 493-E* dated May 1928, recommended Point Montara receive this surplus cast iron tower and lantern from the second district. This cross country transfer was lost to history until 2008, when Colleen MacNeney and her parents Bob and Sandra Shanklin, made the discovery while researching at the USCG Historians office.

After being automated in August 1970, Point Montara suffered a constant barrage of vandalism throughout the decade. In 1980 a lease of the property began with the American Youth Hostels Inc. The California Conservation Corps along with state employees cleared the station of 300-cubic-yards of debris and repaired, sealed and painted the duplex, adding the necessary appliances and furniture needed for operation. Point Montara is still an active aid to navigation, and one of only five lighthouses available for lodging.

Point Montara Light Station
Photo courtesy of The United States Lighthouse Society

RUBICON POINT

Rubicon Point Light
Photograph by Kent Weymouth

The Lake Tahoe Protective Association started to petition the government for navigational lights in 1913. Congress appropriated $900.00 in 1916 to construct a light at Rubicon Point on beautiful Lake Tahoe, north of Emerald Bay in the Sierra Nevada Mountains. Construction of the light took place in 1919, under the direction of the Bureau of Lighthouse Service. Located at over 6,400-feet above sea level, Rubicon Point has the distinction of being built at the highest elevation of any light on a navigable body of water in the world.

Rubicon Point never housed a light-keeper; this small shack like structure is more often mistaken for an outhouse than a lighthouse. The light began its life in 1920, lasting only one year, until the Lighthouse Service abandoned the location and moved the lamp to Sugar Pine Point. The move was made after requests from mariners and the Lake Tahoe Railway and Transportation Company. The lighthouse, acquired in 1929 by the State of California along with 744 acres donated by the D. L. Bliss family, is located in D. L. Bliss State Park. Open to the public via a trail head from late May until the middle of September, the campground is closed during winter. Stabilized in 2001, Rubicon Point light stands as a unique footnote in lighthouse history, preserved for generations to come.

Circular No. 4, of 1894.

Office Light-House Inspector,

San Francisco, Cal., May 7, 1894.

When it is necessary to use the telegraph to communicate with this office on official business, Keepers are directed to indorse upon the message "Official Business, Government Rates" and send them with charges to be collected at this office.

The telegraph is only to be used for such occurrences as an accident to the light, breakdown of fog-signal machinery, prevalence of contageous diseases, death of employes, important wrecks when assistance is required, &c.,&c.   The message should be clear and concise, stating the information in as few words as possible, and to prevent needless expense, the address should be abbrevieted as much as possible.   For illustration, Lighthouse Inspector, San Francisco, is sufficient for the address of a local telegram to the Inspector of the 12th Light-House District, &c., &c.

All messages on personal matters, such as requesting leave of absence, special privileges, &c., &c., must be sent at local rates, and invariably prepaid by the sender.   If an answer is required, it will be sent in the same manner, with charges collect.
                              Henry E. Nichols,
                                   Commander, U.S.N.,
                                        Light-House Inspector.

California Circular number 4 of 1894
Photo courtesy of The United States Lighthouse Society

SAN FRANCISCO BAY LIGHTS

ROE ISLAND

Roe Island sits in the Suisun Bay at the entrance to the Sacramento River, 33 miles from the Golden Gate. The lighthouse was built on pilings due to a low flood plain that would sometimes engulf parts of the island. The station consisted of the lighthouse, oil house, outhouse, and a water house that was fed its running water by a windmill. A fog bell at the end of the pier was struck by machinery, one blow every ten seconds when in use. Its fifth order Fresnel lens came to life on February 16, 1891.

Roe Island light could have remained a minor bookmark in history as a small inland light if it had not been involved peripherally with a significant chapter in American history. What happened next was a catastrophic event that prompted major changes as to how the military dealt with explosives, military training, and race relations.

In November 1942, across the channel from the Roe Island Lighthouse, the Port Chicago ammunitions depot went into operation. Ships were loaded with the necessary ordinance bombs and high explosives to use for the War in the Pacific against Japan. Selecting the location of the depot would be of the utmost importance because seclusion from any population in the event of any explosion was paramount to the decision. Proper safety measures had been taken in the building of the depot. The construction of the appropriate barricades needed on site increased protection against the unthinkable.

From the beginning of the depot's operation, the commanding officer requested additional staffing, proper training, and better facilities for the men, but in a time of war these requests went largely unfulfilled. The best and brightest military personnel went overseas while the new recruits and those deemed less effective for the theatre of war, remained stationed at home. African Americans did not serve as combat troops overseas. They were stationed at home often in dangerous or menial positions. Port Chicago had an insufficient number of officers, all of them were white, and the ammunition loaders of Port Chicago were largely African American. The port lacked a sufficient number of petty officers and those present lacked adequate training. Formal training for the ammunition loaders did not exist. Training was left to hands on demonstrations since a large number of men could not read or write.

On July 17, 1944, 98 enlisted men of the third division were loading the *E. A. Bryan*, with half of the men in the ship and half on the dock. The *Quinault Victory*, a ship only one week old, arrived and anchored outboard opposite and parallel to the inbound *E. A. Bryan*. The crew's 102 enlisted men of the sixth division were rigging the *Quinault Victory* for loading, which was to begin at midnight. A short time after ten there was a sound of cracking wood, then a hollow ring, followed by a bright white flash and a huge explosion sending a column of fire into the air. Within three to six seconds, another even greater blast came from the holds of the *E. A. Bryan*. The combined volume that had been loaded into the ship over the course of four days acted as an enormous bomb sending shock waves felt in a radius of 40 miles. No evidence of the pier or any pilings remained within 400-feet of detonation. Beyond 400-feet, the pier remained, torn from the pilings.

The *E. A. Bryan* and the *Quinault Victory*, two Coast Guard boats, one diesel locomotive, the ships' pier, the joiner shop, a nearby building, and a wharf under construction, were completely destroyed. All the men on the nearby Coast Guard fire barge moored at the east end of the ships' pier were killed and the boat destroyed. When the smoke had cleared, 319 men were lost, 255 men were injured, with 202 of the dead, being black enlisted men. The nearest survivors found were 1,000-feet away, working in the joiner shop. Not badly injured, the men survived despite the destruction of the building. One thousand-yards away, the Roe Island Light Station sustained moderate damage from the blast and ensuing tidal wave.

When the explosion occurred, the *E. A. Bryan* was almost fully loaded with 4,485 tons of ammunition and high explosives. The overall force of the explosion had the combined power of 5,080 tons of ammunition and high explosives, which translates to over 10.1 million pounds of explosives.

Roe Island Light Station
Photo courtesy of The United States Lighthouse Society

Damaged Roe Island Light Station - 1944
Photo courtesy of The United States Lighthouse Society

The *Quinault Victory*, anchored parallel to the *E. A. Bryan*, sat directly in the path of the Roe Island Lighthouse. Blown from the water, broken in pieces, and flipped over, the ship landed the opposite direction 400-yards away. The *Quinault Victory's* location in relation to the *E. A. Bryan* saved the lighthouse from total destruction and the family of Erven Scott from almost certain death.

The Roe Island light-keeper Erven Scott, his wife Bernice, and the assistant keeper were sitting together having a cup of coffee when the explosion hit, shaking the lighthouse violently and blowing out all the windows. Bernice grabbed the two children and Erven ran upstairs to get the baby. From the room's window Erven could see the explosion and mushroom cloud rising in the air. No one at the lighthouse was injured but the damage was severe enough for the Coast Guard to discontinue the use of Roe Island Light in 1945.

After the deactivation of the Roe Island Lighthouse, it sold to a family that used the house as a summer home for several years until the station burned down, torched by arsonists.

CARQUINEZ STRAIT

Located between Suisun Bay and San Pablo Bay, not far inland from the Carquinez Bridge, once sat the Carquinez Strait Lighthouse. Designed for three keepers, the 28-room lighthouse was located off a long pier which extended from the north side of the Carquinez Strait near the mouth of the Napa River, right to the edge of the shallows. Two compressed air siren horns went into operation and a fourth order Fresnel lens first illuminated the river on January 15, 1910.

The water through these channels is very shallow, and the shipping lanes extend far into the river. Ferries commuted between San Francisco and Vallejo, passengers arriving in Vallejo could then take the rail to Napa. With increased traffic along the river it was very important to mark the edge of the shipping lane.

In the interest of navigational safety, the Lighthouse Board first recommended a lighthouse for the Carquinez Strait in 1901, due to the immense amount of commerce passing between San Francisco Bay and Sacramento. The Carquinez Strait Lighthouse remained in service until 1951, replaced with a small beacon at the end of the newly extended pier.

Carquinez Strait Lighthouse
Photo courtesy of The United States Lighthouse Society

Carquinez Strait Lighthouse
Photo courtesy of The United States Lighthouse Society

The structure sold to Robert Hubert, a San Francisco contractor, sometime in the late fifties. Hubert had no luck in finding a company to move the structure so he decided to take it upon himself to do the job. Injured badly after falling from the top of the lighthouse, Hubert was convalescing when vandals destroyed the original Fresnel lens. Upon his recovery, Hubert formed a partnership with Ittsei Nakagawa of El Cerrito, Sokichi Satake of Concord, and Henry Kiyoi of Martinez, and the four had the 150-ton lighthouse barged to Elliot Cove, just over a mile from its original home in 1955.

When the fog signal and tower were removed from the lighthouse, this elegant structure began to fall into disrepair. A restoration movement during the marina development brought the grand structure back from the brink of disaster. The Glen Cove Marina now acts as home to this, one of California's largest lighthouses.

MARE ISLAND

Mare Island is an isthmus located across from Vallejo at the entrance to the Carquinez Strait, stretching the length of the eastern end of San Pablo Bay.

General Mariano Vallejo, a member of the constitutional convention that led to the forming of California as a state, was transporting horses across the Carquinez Strait on a barge when it sank. The general's favorite horse had been aboard and was feared lost. Later, his prized white mare appeared grazing on the banks of the nearby isthmus, leaving it forever known as "Mare Island"

Mare Island was the location of the first Pacific Fleet base located near the mouth of the Napa River. The charming wooden Victorian light station stood perched on a hill and was built in a similar style to neighboring East Brother light station less than 13 miles away. A point south of the dwelling, chosen for the fog signal building, had a retaining wall of rock built above the high-water mark, surrounding a graded plateau. From the boat landing, two inclines each with a turntable, car, and windlass were set up, one to the fog signal and another to the light-keeper's dwelling.

The lighthouse, completed in July 1873, did not begin operation immediately due to a lack of water. For the next 25 years, water posed the primary challenge for the station and attempts at digging a well were without success. A suitable water source for Mare Island continued to elude workers. A new water-tank installed in 1877 proved insufficient, so a dam 13-feet long and seven-feet high added to the station, created a water-catchment area. Water filtered through gravel and flowed through a pipe to the cisterns, but water was still in short supply. A watershed added to the station still did not fulfill the water needs. Therefore, the city of Vallejo laid a pipe across the strait, underwater from Vallejo to the island. However, the city discontinued its use in 1898, because the anchors of vessels crossing through the straits had damaged the pipe so badly. The pipe had moved so far out of place that it would have been costly and futile to replace the entire line. Finally, the naval authorities on the island laid a large main connecting the Navy yard to the Vallejo waterworks, an arrangement to lay a two-inch pipe from the Navy yard to the lighthouse, effectively connected it to a constant water supply.

In its brief lifetime, Mare Island lighthouse had three women appointed as light-keepers, Mrs. Theresa C. Watson, the light-keeper from 1873-1881, served with her daughter, Miss B. M. Watson, appointed first assistant keeper in December 1876.

Commander Charles J. McDougal, Inspector of the Twelfth Lighthouse District, drowned when the small boat he was operating capsized. McDougal was rowing from the Light Tender Manzanita to the

Cape Mendocino Lighthouse and was weighted down with the payroll he was delivering. George Dewey, a classmate of Inspector McDougal at the Naval Academy, arranged for McDougal's wife Kate, left with four children and a small pension, to serve at Mare Island. Appointed light-keeper in December 1881, Kate C. McDougal remained until the closure of the station in 1916, 35 years later.

The 1906 earthquake damaged the fourth order lens, which was repaired by resetting the loose prisms and replacing the braces. Also damaged by the earthquake were three chimneys that were rebuilt and outfitted with galvanized-iron tops.

The Lighthouse Board felt that the Carquinez Strait was a better location for a light and decided to end the operation at Mare Island in 1916, upon completing the automation of the fog signal. Although abandoned in July 1917, the station remained until being torn down in the 1930s.

Mare Island Light Station - September 1908
Photo courtesy of The United States Lighthouse Society

OAKLAND HARBOR

Oakland Lighthouse
Photo courtesy of The United States Lighthouse Society

Just south of the Embarcadero and Jack London Square is where what is left of the Oakland Harbor Lighthouse can be found. Moved to its current location in 1965, the Oakland Lighthouse opened as Quinn's restaurant and bar in 1984. Explore this historic structure, enjoy a cocktail on the second floor, and look out over the Oakland Estuary and Coast Guard Island. Quinn's offers a unique lighthouse experience unlike any other in northern California.

Sitting at the entrance to the Oakland Estuary and San Antonio Creek, in 13-feet of water, the Oakland light first began its operation on January 27, 1890. Sitting upon 11 piles, driven 14-feet into the bottom of the bay, was a wooden frame dwelling with an iron lantern house. A 3,500 pound bell was mounted on the surrounding deck just feet from the light-keepers' bedroom. Duty on the light was isolated despite being located between two of the largest cities in northern California. Rowing kept the keepers in shape and was their chief mode of transportation. They rowed to town for their supplies and mail. They rowed to service the eight-day lens lantern on the south jetty. They rowed to the red lantern one mile to the east or to any other destination that required leaving the station. The lighthouse always moved and rocked with the tides creating a slight sway that was visible even to the passerby.

Hermann and Freda Engel, stationed at the Oakland Lighthouse at the turn of the century, were present on December 1, 1900, when the steamer *Newark* accidentally rammed the lighthouse breaking a piling, splintering timbers, and knocking other pilings askew. The *Newark* was 294-feet long and had paddle wheels 42-feet in diameter, possibly the largest ever used on a steamer. According to Norma Engel in her book "Three Beams of Light;" the Engel's and keeper Charles McCarthy were in the kitchen having toast and coffee when Freda looked up and said, "Look what's coming." Both keepers gazed in astonishment to see the steamer headed right for the lighthouse. The lookout on the *Newark* had seen the light but not fast enough for the helmsman to turn away in time. When the steamer hit, the captain of the ship came storming onto the deck and began yelling obscenities at the lighthouse as if it had somehow purposely gotten in the way. The damage from the collision had left the light a little worse for the wear. Only 18 days passed after the collision before all repairs to the lighthouse were complete.

Even before the *Newark* struck, the lighthouse was undergoing a more sinister demise. The structure was being rendered unstable due to damage created by marine borers-shipworms. Evidence of the worms was first reported only four years after construction. Even 2,000 tons of stone quarried on Yerba Buena (Goat) Island and poured around the pilings for additional stability, proved futile. In 1902, the Secretary of the Treasury stated in a letter to the Speaker of the House and recorded in the 1902 annual report to Congress, "Its wooden pile foundation has deteriorated to such an extent as to render it liable to collapse at any time."

Traffic had been on a steady increase at the harbor with ferryboats making regular trips at night, so the need for a light was imperative. Congress approved appropriations for the construction of a new light station in Oakland in 1902. Beginning operation on July 11, 1903, the new Oakland Lighthouse still sat in the water off the pier, but it was larger and supported by steel cylinders, four-feet in diameter with three pine piles inserted, driven to bedrock, and then filled with cement to prevent a similar occurrence. The building was two stories, with balconies surrounding each level. The first level was used for storage with the upper level housing the keepers, and the fog signal machinery. The lantern room housed the fifth order Fresnel lens that topped off the structure.

The pier was extended out farther to encompass the lighthouse, making it easier for the light-keepers and their families, who would no longer need to use a rowboat to access the lighthouse. The pier brought the central Pacific Railroad and local ferry service quite literally to the keepers' backyard, with the stations located on the pier just yards from their door.

Myron Edgington, the last light-keeper of the Oakland Harbor Light, opened the lighthouse to visitors sometime in the 1950s, unfortunately, his skills as a marketer did not equal his skills as a light-keeper. The lighthouse was so close to downtown Oakland, the fog signal could be clearly heard, yet it would be six years before anyone showed up for a tour. Luckily, when someone did show up, he was a reporter for the Oakland Tribune. That fateful visitor spread the word, giving the little beacon on the pier a last burst of glory and making it quite well known. Oakland school children glimpsed into a dying past, marveling at the efficiency with which Edgington performed his duties. The brass was always polished, the paint glistened, and the light operated impeccably.

The Oakland light remained in operation for 62 years before deactivation in 1965, when it was barged to its current location. In 1966, an automatic beacon installed near the original location of the lighthouse took the place of the historic lantern room, which then found a new life at the Santa Cruz memorial lighthouse. The lantern room and lens were subsequently relocated in 1996, to the Mobile Lighthouse in Alabama.

Oakland Lighthouse
Photo courtesy of The United States Lighthouse Society

EAST BROTHER ISLAND

The East Brother Light Station (EBLS) offers a unique experience for the lighthouse enthusiast, traveler, or romantic couple, as one of two bed and breakfast inns to be found among California's lighthouses. One of the most fully restored light stations in the state; EBLS offers a restful and relaxing experience unlike any other. The station, accessible only by boat, has no way for the casual visitor to drop by. Reservations are required for admittance to this magnificent station.

The trip from the harbor to EBLS is made in the station boat. Passengers disembark onto the wharf after the boat has been hoisted up and out of the water. The first building encountered when arriving on the island is the fog signal building. Beautifully maintained, housing two great engines that drive the bellowing bass diaphones that once warned ship captains during a dense fog. The fog signal, is still fired up for guests on occasion, and has the characteristic deep bass that seems to vibrate the very island itself. The monotonous high pitch tone of the horn on West Brother Island is currently used as the fog signal. Water flowing past the island, is fed from the Sacramento, Napa, and Petaluma rivers, as well as small tributaries that empty into San Pablo Bay. Currents are so visibly strong through the channel that from the station the island appears to be speeding through the bay.

In 1867, President Andrew Johnson set aside the Brother and Sister Islands for the military. Situated in the San Francisco Bay off the coast of Richmond's Point San Pablo, East Brother measures less than an acre. Located just yards away, West Brother Island is host only to the birds of the bay, giving the gulls, pelicans, and cormorants a place to perch. The Brother Islands lie less than two miles south of the Sister Islands, located on the east side of the San Pablo Strait, a two-mile-wide waterway that connects San Pablo Bay to San Francisco Bay.

The Lighthouse Board requested the building of a lighthouse on Point San Pablo in 1870, for which Congress made appropriations in March 1871. However, the landowner refused to sell the property, so the government began condemnation proceedings, which awarded the landowner a sum of $4,000, which he rejected, appealing to the California Supreme Court.

In January 1873, boat captains in the area, so displeased with the delays, sent a petition to the lighthouse inspector proposing to build the lighthouse on East Brother Island, already owned by the government. The Board earnestly agreed with the proposition, placing the lighthouse on the island would be advantageous. Locating it closer to the shipping lanes would allow for greater visibility. The most important disadvantage to building on the island was the lack of fresh water.

Contractors Monroe and Burns of San Francisco were hired by the

East Brother Island Light Station
Photo courtesy of the United States Lighthouse Society

Federal Government to blast away the top of the island in preparation for the construction of the station. The crew built a retaining wall around the island, and then used the blasting remains of broken sandstone to back fill between the two.

The lighthouse had mortared bricks built into the outer walls to reinforce the wooden-framed construction. This acted as a partial sound barrier from the fog signal, and helped to insulate the house against the natural forces of the bay. The house, a six-room dwelling, was designed for three keepers. The upstairs was split between the first assistant and his family, and one unmarried second assistant, housed in a loft above the kitchen and dining room. The principal keeper and his family lived on the first floor.

Rain water flowed from the building roofs, down gutters and collected in the rain-shed catchment that covered the majority of the island. Water was fed to the cistern, which was covered by a dome in the center of the station. The red roofs of the station were painted with a toxic lead paint which contaminated the water with each rainfall. Purification of the water by boiling was not effective, so powdered chalk was stirred into the cistern after each rainfall to neutralize the lead. The catchment system worked quite well, and was able to capture 5,000 gallons for every one inch of rainfall. To prepare for the following rainy season the cistern would be pumped out and cleaned each fall.

The island started rocking early on the morning of April 18, 1906, when the great San Francisco earthquake struck. The light-keeper John Stenmark recorded in the logbook

> "A heavy earthquake this morning at 5:15 A.M. Lenses of the light broken and glassware broke and everything of glass broke. Doors open of themselves and the whole island rocking. All the lenses broke." The following day Stenmark's entry read, "S. F. burning fearfully at 9 P. M."
>
> *East Brother; History of a Light Station, by Frank Perry*

No structural damage to the station took place, but the residents, like their neighboring bay keepers, could only watch across the water as San Francisco burned.

In June of 1907, the steamer *A. C. Freese,* while towing the steamer *Leader* and two barges, was traveling south through the narrow channel. Crew members stationed on board had fallen asleep and were unaware that the currents had moved them off course. As the steamer moved past the island, the *Leader* struck the wharf with full force snapping the tow ropes and subjecting the wharf to major damage. The ship had run into the pilings, destroying them and damaging the boathouse as well.

In 1934, electricity made its way to East Brother Light Station when crews submerged a power cable between East Brother and Point San Pablo. In the early morning of March 4, 1940, the worst event in the light station's history took place. The electrical cable connecting the station to the mainland was disconnected for repairs and the light was being temporarily produced using a gasoline-powered generator. Keeper Willard Miller needed to refill a kerosene lantern, and while filling a small container, he stepped back and accidentally knocked over the lantern. Immediately the kerosene spilled from the lantern, spread across the wooden floor of the boathouse, and set the structure aflame. As the flames began to spread, Miller attempted to close the spigot of the 50-gallon drum, but his hand and arm were set ablaze. Grabbing a fire extinguisher, Miller attempted to put out the flames but the kerosene soaked wooden floor quickly became a raging inferno. Miller turned and ran up the tramway to the island and just as he reached the top, the first drum exploded, followed by four more explosions that sent a plume of flames 100-feet in the air. Miller barely escaped with his life, unharmed except for the burns he suffered to his right hand.

The explosion awakened Earl and Lillian Snodgrass who were asleep in the lighthouse. Leaping out of bed to look out their window, they saw flames billowing up from behind the fog signal building. Racing downstairs, they found that the fire had already set the picket fence aflame and was moving to engulf the east side of the fog-signal building. Earl Snodgrass and Willard Miller grabbed the water hose in an attempt to contain the blaze, but as the fire reached additional drums, more explosions rocked the island. The men watered down what they could of the side of the fog signal building and its roof, but the low water pressure on the island hindered their attempts.

On the pier at San Pablo, a night watchman witnessed the explosion and called the Richmond Fire Department, who alerted the Coast Guard to the situation. A cutter, dispatched at full speed, still took 35 minutes to arrive at the island. For an hour, the three island residents had been fighting the fire. When the Coast Guard arrived, they used the cutter's water pump to douse the flames, but another hour passed before the fire was extinguished. Destruction at the station included the boathouse, four boats, the wharf, and the tramway. The fog signal building survived the

East Brother Island Light Station
Photo courtesy of the United States Lighthouse Society

fire, although badly scorched.

The Navy began filling the cistern with water supplied from a cutter in 1946, eliminating the use of the watershed. Other changes soon came to the light station. The resident keepers were discontinued and replaced with a two-man Coast Guard crew, rotated every 48 hours. Lighthouse life all over America was changing as the Coast Guard looked for ways to increase efficiency and decrease operating costs.

In 1967, plans to automate the station included the demolition of the lighthouse, replacing it with a light on a tower. An effort to save the historical structures on the island, started by the Contra Costa Shoreline Parks Committee in 1968, had the City Council, Contra Costa County Board of Supervisors, and the Richmond Planning Commission pass a resolution asking the Coast Guard not to raze the buildings. The Coast Guard agreed and informed the agencies that it would donate or lease the island to any government agency willing to conserve it as a historical landmark. Although several agencies showed interest, none was willing or able to shoulder the expense of maintaining the structures.

Luckily, when automation came to the lighthouse in 1969, it escaped the wrecking ball. Instead a tall chain-link fence erected at the dock worked to prevent entrance to the island and deter vandalism. The Contra Costa Shoreline Parks Committee with the cooperation of the Coast Guard allowed reporters from a San Francisco television station to tour the island in 1970. A plea went out for public support to help save the lighthouse, which led to a flood of telephone calls, telegrams, and letters to the committee wanting to help preserve the light station. The addition of EBLS to the National Register of Historic Places in 1971 prevented the demolition of the lighthouse. No money for a restoration was available from any agency, so the light station remained largely unchanged for almost ten years.

Formed in 1979, East Brother Light Station, Inc., a non-profit group created to restore the lighthouse to its original state and open it to the public, began the task. The organization leased the station from the Coast Guard, and with private donations, government grants, and countless hours of volunteer labor, completed the restoration of the structures on the island. The rain shed had deteriorated beyond all repairs necessitating complete replacement, so the rain captured could fill the cistern for use as the islands water supply. A crew from the California Conservation Corps worked for six weeks removing the old concrete. Over 100 tons of concrete ready-mix was barged to the island, mixed, and poured into the 9,000 square-foot rain shed. East Brother Light Station now serves as a bed & breakfast and remains a popular destination.

SOUTHAMPTON SHOALS

Southampton Shoals Lighthouse
Photo courtesy of The United States Lighthouse Society

Tinsley Island, located in the San Joaquin Delta, is the only island in the United States to be owned by a yacht club. Only members of the St. Francis Yacht Club are able to visit the island, and stay in the Southampton Shoals Lighthouse.

This private island is not visible from shore, and through ingenious design is invisible from the water. Tinsley Island is an island within an island, with only three small channels in which to enter. As we entered the channel surrounding the inner island, the vision slowly came creeping into view, the beautiful Southampton Shoals Lighthouse.

A plaque commemorating the acquisition of Tinsley Island greets visitors as they enter. Lining the walls are aerial pictures of the island with the lighthouse in various stages of its move from the San Francisco Bay to Tinsley Island. Other nautical items dot the room giving it a clubhouse like atmosphere. The main room has a piano, table, and a couple of love seats to give guests a room to relax and enjoy the peaceful surroundings. Upstairs is very homey with cheery décor throughout the five rooms and three baths. The cupola may lack a lens and light but it opens up to an impressive view of the island and the delta. From the lantern room the unique dormers and interesting rain gutters of this beautiful Victorian structure can be seen.

Southampton Shoals, located in the San Francisco Bay, measures a third of a mile wide and two miles long. The shoals run along the eastern shipping channel, located a little over a mile northeast of Angel Island. When the Santa Fe Railroad began a new ferry service from Point Richmond to San Francisco, the path ran just to the southeast edge of the shoals. The shoals also posed a threat to tugboats, riverboats, and yachts of the bay. So a light was planned to help navigate ships away from the dangerous shoals.

In 1905, the three-story Southampton Shoals Lighthouse began its tenure in the bay. The structure was built on 11 concrete cylinders encased in steel and driven into the shoals. A fifth order Fresnel lens topped off the lighthouse, and a bell in excess of 3,000 pounds served as the fog signal.

In the first year of operation, the pilings slipped. Crews distributed 1,000 tons of rocks around the pilings to help secure the foundation. A few months later the 1906 earthquake occurred, shifting the lighthouse again. For the remainder of its life on the bay, some of the pilings would be as much as 11 degrees out of plumb.

In 1932, Ole Lunden and his wife were stationed on Southampton Shoals. Across the bay Albert Joost and his wife were stationed at Yerba Buena Light Station, and had taken to lighthouse life. After being stationed at East Brother Light Station and Yerba Buena, they were ready for a new challenge. Albert Joost asked Ole Lunden if he would be interested in trading assignments: he and his wife would move to Southampton Shoals, and Lunden could take his wife and move to Yerba Buena. Lunden jumped at the chance for the two to live on solid ground again and agreed to make the change. After the appropriate approvals from their superiors, the couples changed locations. This was a fateful decision that led to one of the most tragic events in California lighthouse history.

On December 23, 1935, the assistant keeper of Southampton Shoals had gone ashore. Mrs. Joost was in the lighthouse, and Albert Joost was on the southwest corner of the veranda performing maintenance on the radio set and antenna. While using a blowtorch to heat the soldering iron, (a common practice at the time) an explosion engulfed Joost and the southwest corner of the lighthouse. Mrs. Joost rushed to aid her husband who had entered the lighthouse aflame to obtain the fire extinguisher. She found him in the hall, and together they extinguished his flames, and then put out the fire that threatened the lighthouse. Severely burned, Albert Joost now found himself in a difficult spot. After lowering the station launch with the help of his wife, he insisted that she stay to tend the light. Albert Joost then managed by himself to row to Angel Island and the nearest medical attention. Upon reaching Fort McDowell he was immediately taken in a military boat to the Marine Hospital in San Francisco.

When the news reached Lighthouse District Superintendent Captain Harry Rhodes, he got word to light-keeper Spellman at Yerba Buena Light Station, to get to Southampton Shoals immediately and take charge until he was relieved. Upon arriving at the lighthouse, keeper Spellman relieved Mrs. Joost of her duty, allowing her to get to the hospital so she could sit at the side of her husband. Albert Joost died two days later on Christmas day.

The next day upon inspection, all evidence pointed to the southwest corner of the lighthouse, near the keepers' quarters as to where the fire had started. Burnt clothing pieces led a trail to the water tank, where Joost, had been unable to get any water. He then headed inside leaving scorched walls and door casings. In the hall, a large scorched area where Joost fell left a burnt semi circle and more clothing pieces. A dedicated light-keeper had given his life to the service, and his wife, knowing the importance of his role stood by the light and never left the post.

The decision to replace the grand old light with a small-automated beacon came in 1960. The new light would be capable of shining a brighter light and would never require a light-keeper. The job of removing

Southampton Shoals Lighthouse, moving day July 6, 1960
Photo courtesy of The United States Lighthouse Society

Southampton Shoals Replacement Beacon
Photo courtesy of The United States Lighthouse Society

the lighthouse fell to the Healy-Tibbets Construction Company. John Marhens, president of the company, decided it would be wasteful if not disrespectful to destroy the historic lighthouse, so he donated it to the St. Francis Yacht Club.

Smith-Rice Company and Crowley Tugboat Company teamed up to do the moving. The structure was lifted off the pilings by two huge barge-borne derricks and then lowered gently onto a third barge, which carried it up the San Joaquin River to Tinsley Island. The derrick operators were so skillful in moving the three-story 150-ton structure that not even a pane of glass was broken. All told, the project cost St. Francis Yacht Club about $3,000, a great deal for the Yacht Club and a small price to pay to save this historic structure.

The lens from the Southampton Shoals Lighthouse is on display in the Angel Island visitor's center, not far from its original home. The pilings on Southampton Shoals still protrude from the waters off Angel Island. There is a small platform with a light mounted on a pole that takes the place of the glorious house on the bay.

YERBA BUENA

Separating Yerba Buena Island from Treasure Island is the Oakland San Francisco Bay Bridge. Both islands provide a wonderful view of Alcatraz and San Francisco. Only Treasure Island is accessible to the public and even then, it is on a limited scale. For many years, Yerba Buena was the Coast Guard headquarters for the Bay Area's Aids to Navigation Team. Still an operating military base, the island and lighthouse are off limits to the public. The lighthouse grounds have magnificent views of San Francisco and Oakland and fabulous landscaping that surrounds the meticulously maintained light-keepers' house and light tower. The fog signal building is a small museum of sorts, housing past photos and a few historic artifacts. Yerba Buena became the home of the Lighthouse Service depot in 1873, after moving from Mare Island. The small light tower sits down the hill from the light-keepers' dwelling, (now the Pacific area commander's residence, also used to entertain dignitaries). This is the most beautiful existing lighthouse dwelling left standing in California.

On October 1, 1875, the unique, 25-foot tall octagonal lighthouse first shone its light from a fifth order Fresnel lens (previously used in the Yaquina Bay Lighthouse in Oregon). The station's fog signal was established in 1874, using the bell previously in service at Point Conception. The bell, replaced the following year with a steam whistle, was then used as a backup. Water needed to create steam for the whistle, came from a spring near the buoy depot. In 1880, the fog bell was again transferred, this time to Fort Point, replacing a smaller bell, which was then transferred to Yerba Buena and used as a backup for the steam whistle.

The water supply to the station had to be hand pumped by one of the two keepers. This created concerns that during a prolonged period of fog, there might not be an adequate water supply. An additional water tank was installed along with a new pump and boiler, in the hope of supplying water for the entire station, and not just the steam whistle. Now in the event of a fire, there would be enough water pressure to reach any part of the depot. Despite the efforts, a drought in 1884 caused the well that had supplied the water for the station to run dry, forcing the service to use harbor water boats to fill the tanks.

In 1933, a tunnel was bored through Yerba Buena Island to prepare a connecting road for the Bay Bridge, between Oakland and San Francisco.

Tenders based at Yerba Buena were dispatched to each of the lighthouses along the coast every three to four months, to bring keepers supplies, books, and mail. But when the tenders arrived, so did the lighthouse inspector, ready to go over the station from top to bottom.

Automated in 1958, Yerba Buena Lighthouse is closed to the public and visible only from the water.

Yerba Buena Light Station
Photo courtesy of The United States Lighthouse Society

LIGHTHOUSE ON GOAT ISLAND IN SAN FRANCISCO HARBOR

Yerba Buena Light Station - 1908
Photo courtesy of The United States Lighthouse Society

ALCATRAZ ISLAND LIGHTHOUSE

One of San Francisco's most popular destination points was also one of America's most notorious prisons, and now one of our most popular National Parks. Sadly, more people are interested in learning about the prison's brief infamous residents, including Al Capone, Machine Gun Kelly, and Robert Stroud (The Birdman of Alcatraz) than learning about lighthouse lore.

Visiting the island begins with a short ferry ride from Pier 41. Reservations for the ferry are necessary, as this trip is very popular. Alcatraz has a self-guided tour, allowing the visitor to explore the island with more freedom than any inmate ever experienced while living on the Rock. Still maintained by the United States Coast Guard, the stark cement lighthouse tower stands at the entrance to the prison. No doubt this mighty tower will impress any lighthouse enthusiast, yet goes unnoticed by most visitors.

The prison is much smaller than most would assume. The main prison originally housed 348 cells, all sharing common walls with their neighboring cell. Each cell measured five-feet wide by nine-feet long, and they were stacked three stories high. According to the National Park Service, 12 cells were removed to accommodate the stairs installed at the end of each cell block. The cell blocks were situated with cell block "A" on the right as you enter the prison and "D" block to the left. Cell block "A" was used primarily as a storage area, but was occasionally used for isolating troublemakers. Cell block "D" consisted of 36 isolation cells and 6 solitary confinement cells. One of these cells (the strip cell or "Oriental") had no sink or toilet, only a hole in the ground that was flushed by a guard from a remote area. These six cells were kept in complete darkness behind a solid metal door. If a guard felt a prisoner was behaving well, and was compelled to reward him, he could do so by opening a small cover to allow light in. A narrow utility corridor containing the electrical and plumbing for each cell separated each row of cells in the block.

In 1850, President Millard Fillmore reserved Alcatraz Island for government use, along with other San Francisco Bay Area land. In 1851, Alcatraz was chosen as the first location to build a lighthouse on the west coast. It would share the same Cape Cod style as the next six California lighthouses. Stone, bricks, and lime were the only local building materials used. Lumber, equipment, and workmen came from the east around the Horn on the Barkentine sailing ship *Oriole*, although some of the men came west by way of Panama.

Work began in December 1852, and was completed by the following July, at a cost of just under $15,000.

Appointed in April 1853, Michael Cassin became the first light-keeper of Alcatraz. However, Cassin did not go to work right away. When the lens arrived in October 1853, the funds for installation were not available, so the job had to wait. When the new light on Alcatraz Island began its operation on June 1, 1854, the third order lens, fueled by lard, was visible for 14 miles.

Protecting San Francisco from foreign invasion was the job of the United States Army, who shared the island with the lighthouse. By 1858, fortification on the summit had surrounded the lighthouse. In 1883, a new bell, weighing 3,340 pounds, was cast at the Mare Island Navy yard using the old bell. The new bell was then placed in a new structure erected 15-feet closer to the beach, increasing the range of the bell. In 1901, a small frame structure was erected on the northern end of the island to house the clockwork apparatus used to strike the fog bell. The new electricity allowed the light-keeper the ability to start and stop the striking mechanism from his quarters. The original third order lens was replaced in 1902 with a forth order lens. At the same time, a new fog signal striking apparatus was installed that hit the bell harder, producing a more effective signal.

At 5:12 a.m. April 18, 1906, San Francisco woke abruptly to 48 seconds of rolling and swaying, as the great quake shook the city. In the bay, Alcatraz did not go unscathed; the stone tower cracked, and the chimneys of the quarters were destroyed. Like their fellow light-keepers around the Bay, those on Alcatraz could only watch from across the water. Dam-

Original Alcatraz Lighthouse
Photo courtesy of The United States Lighthouse Society

age from the quake was severe but not catastrophic, and then the fires began. On Alcatraz, the light-keeper wrote in the keepers' log: "violent and continued earthquake-San Francisco on fire-people on beach-is this the end of the world? Prisoner going crazy-terrible seeing S.F. from here. Lighthouse walls-cracking." The fires would last for three days.

In 1908, the military authorities decided to construct a new prison on Alcatraz Island, one that would require land occupied by the light station. The new lighthouse on Alcatraz would be constructed using reinforced concrete and would house a fourth order Fresnel lens. The new 84-foot tower rose just 50-feet outside the prison walls. The new lighthouse tower and light-keepers' dwellings were built for under $35,000. The lens rotated on a series of 21, 3/8 inch balls encased in a cage, supported by four stanchions. An 80 pound weight at the end of a rope powered the mechanism much like a grandfather clock. It took four hours for the weight to complete the drop, before keepers' had to rewind the clockworks. Three, two story dwellings surrounded the tower and were painted white with brown trim and red roofs. The new tower was equipped with electricity, which also powered the new sirens located on either side of the island.

With no school on the island, the children of the light-keepers took a daily boat trip into San Francisco for their education. Keepers' and their wives also had to take a boat to shop or carry out other chores in the city. Upon each departure and arrival, the boat would be searched and the passengers counted. Keepers would wait at the lighthouse until a horn was sounded signaling them that it was safe to take the walk down to the dock.

The lighthouse was connected to the light-keepers dwellings, so they could maintain the light even during lock downs, when they had to bolt the windows and lock the doors. Light-keepers were required to wear the Coast Guard uniform to be easily identified, and were restricted to the lighthouse area for safety reasons; no one would be safe wandering around this island unannounced. When the fog signal had to be serviced, the keeper would inform the guards of the path they were going to take to the sirens, and the time they would leave. The guards would use hand signals to direct the wickies to their destination, letting them know from the towers when it was safe to proceed. Keepers could only cross the prison yard when convicts were not present, and guards would open the electronic gates to pass, via a remote control in the watch towers. From the watch towers, the guards would often be the first to spot fog, as it rolled in through the Golden Gate. They often called the keepers to inform them, so they could throw the switch that would start the fog signal.

The Alcatraz Island Light Station was automated in 1963. The fourth order lens was replaced by a powerful rotating aero bea-

Alcatraz Lighthouse
Photo courtesy of The United States Lighthouse Society

con and Norman Fornachon, the last light-keeper of the oldest lighthouse on the Pacific Coast, was taken from the island.

In the early 1970s, Indians occupying the island destroyed the keepers' dwellings at the light station and damaged the tower. The tower, with its rotating aero-beacon, still remains in use. The fog signals located on the north and south ends of the island are controlled by an electronic fog detector. The fourth order lens installed in 1902 is on display in the Park Service Museum on the island.

ANGEL ISLAND STATE PARK

Located only three and a half miles from San Francisco, Angel Island is nevertheless a world away. Boats arrive on the northwestern side of the island at beautiful Ayala cove. This cove is the entry point for most visitors to this charming get away isle, and has a sprawling green lawn surrounded by lush vegetation. Facilities include bicycle rentals, a small gift-shop, a café/snack bar and a tram tour, but check ahead as to their availability, as schedules differ throughout the year. In the off season, transportation is limited to walking, but for those bringing a bicycle, the whole island is open to explore. The Immigration Station can be found along the route to Point Blunt, which sits on the northern end of the island. Once considered the west coast equivalent to Ellis Island, this historic area has just undergone a major restoration. Rebuilt as it stood in 1910, the station is now used as a museum and interpretive center, like many of the islands other historic buildings. Quite a few structures on the island are in need of restoration, but it is a thrill to see the preservation of others.

The road that winds around the entire perimeter of the island was originally created using serpentine rock quarried from a hill on the southwest corner of the island.

Point Blunt, one of the three Angel Islands lights, was never actually a lighthouse in the true sense of the word, but a modern step in the evolution

Point Blunt, Angel Island
Photo courtesy of The United States Lighthouse Society

Point Knox, Angel Island
Photo courtesy of The United States Lighthouse Society

of lights as they are now used. The compound is closed to the public. The light building is home to two ten inch beacons, and the foghorns used to warn ships during the bays notorious foggy summer mornings.

The view from this charming little island is breathtaking: Berkeley, Oakland, Treasure Island, Yerba Buena Island, Alcatraz Island, San Francisco, Marin, Sausalito, Belvedere Island, Tiburon, Richmond, Brooks Island, Albany, the Bay Bridge, the Golden Gate Bridge, and the Richmond-San Rafael Bridge can all be seen from Angel Island.

Angel Island holds true riches for the lighthouse enthusiast historically but not for those looking for actual lighthouses to view. Point Knox is the original Angel Island lighthouse but all that remains is part of the foundation and Juliet's bell. The stairs that led down to the point have been removed, and there is no safe route onto the point. Point Knox has no public access and no direct visibility from the road or open trails. You can see the bell in the distance from the edge of the water at the west garrison of Camp Reynolds, as you look toward San Francisco.

Juliet E. Nichols, one of California's finest light-keepers, was appointed to Point Knox in 1902. On July 2, 1906, a heavy fog crept into the bay. After a short time the automatic striking mechanism for the fog bell stopped working. Knowing her duty and the importance of the bell to all seafaring men, Juliet picked up a hammer and began to pound on the bell, twice every 15 seconds. Time passed and Juliet continued to sound the bell as the fog blanketed the bay. When the fog lifted, Juliet had rung the bell by hand for 20 hours and 35 minutes. Two days later when fog filled the bay, the mechanism broke again. Barely recuperated, Juliet used a hammer again to manually strike the bell through the entire night. Juliet Nichols was commended for her actions by George Putnam, the Commissioner of Lighthouses. Juliet retired from her post at Point Knox in 1914, and lived in the Oakland hills until she died in 1947 at 88 years of age.

Point Stuart, the last of the three Angel Island lights, is just a small wooden structure visible only from the water. Located on the southwestern tip of the island, Point Stuart sits on a cliff and the building is in disrepair and unsafe. The current replacement; an automated lighted buoy moored just below Point Stuart can be seen from the ferry as it passes. Point Stuart's access, overgrown with vegetation that covers the rotting stairs makes the entire area very unsafe. Point Stuart is behind locked United States Coast Guard gates and is off limits to the public.

Point Stuart, Angel Island
Photograph by Kent Weymouth

FORT POINT

Fort Point had taken eight years to construct and was the only brick fort west of the Mississippi. The fort, modeled after South Carolina's Fort Sumter, was built with outer walls five-to-seven-feet thick, consisting of over eight million bricks. Completed in February 1861, by the U.S. Army Corps of Engineers, Fort Point had the important task of preventing a hostile fleet from entering the San Francisco Bay. Built using the latest technologies Fort Point was an engineering marvel, and the most advanced fort of its time.

Part of the Golden Gate National Recreation Area, Fort Point is nestled below the southern anchorage of the Golden Gate Bridge. The lighthouse is located on the roof but is no longer in operation (a beacon is located on the northwestern outer side of the fort, close to the water). The fort is open to explore, although there is no admittance to the tower itself. None of the original keepers' dwellings remain, but some of the buildings that were part of the nearby Life Saving Station sit just south of the point.

San Francisco, known for its biting cold, has wind that rushes through the Golden Gate from the open ocean. On top of the fort, where the lighthouse resides, the cold can be excruciating.

This is not the first light to shine from Fort Point, nor is it the second, this is the third major lighthouse constructed on the promontory within the first dozen years. The original lighthouse, known then as Battery Point, was built in 1852, and was only the second lighthouse to be completed in California. It also became the first California Lighthouse to be torn down. While waiting for the Fresnel lens to arrive from France, unbeknownst to the Lighthouse Board, the Army Corps of Engineers had chosen the spot to build San Francisco's primary fortification against invasion. Just three months after completing the first Fort Point light, the structure came down to make way for the new fort. When the Fresnel lens did arrive, it was shipped to Point Pinos where it remains in use today.

Constructed at the expense of the Army, the second lighthouse at Fort Point was a frame tower, 36-feet in height and built on the narrow ledge between the fort and the seawall. The new lighthouse began its operation using a fifth order fixed lens in March 1855, but by 1863, the strong currents rushing through the bay had begun to undermine the shore near the fort. The Lighthouse Board secured permission to relocate the light, and the lighthouse at Fort Point was razed again, facilitating the construction of a new granite block seawall.

The third lighthouse is the structure found atop the fort today. First shone in January of 1864, the new structure stands 27-feet tall. The light is a nine sided tower mounted at the top of a spiral staircase, painted white and capped by a black lantern room. A small concrete oil house constructed

Fort Point second lighthouse at left and current tower on roof behind dwelling
Photo courtesy of the United States Lighthouse Society

on the roof near the tower housed the fuel.

The keepers' dwellings resided on the nearby bluff, with a footbridge spanning the chasm to the fort. During storms and rough weather, the wind would rush through the gorge with such ferocity that it made crossing the bridge a hazard. So the keepers would often take the path down and enter from the ground level as they had done before the advent of the bridge.

Light-keeper James Rankin contracted with the U.S. Lighthouse Service, and spent his first assignment at East Brother Light Station in San Pablo Bay. Rankin arrived at Fort Point in August 1878, and served as the head keeper for 41 years, one of the longest serving keepers on the west coast. Commended by the Lighthouse Board upon his retirement, Rankin was credited for saving 18 lives at Fort Point, the last two when he was 77 years old and just a year before he retired.

In 1880, the copper bell used as the fog signal at Yerba Buena, transferred to Fort Point. Mounted on the side of the Bastion, the bell had a small building constructed around its clockwork machinery. To reach the bell, the keeper had to climb down a ladder from the roof of the fort to the bell's platform. The bell was located directly under a battery of canons and keepers had to risk their lives to get to the small outcropping.

The steamer *Rio de Janeiro* (see Mile Rocks) sank after striking the Fort Point Shoal, resulting in a loss of over 100 lives. The Lighthouse Board stated in the annual report to Congress in 1901 that the shipwreck "might not have occurred if an efficient signal had been in operation here."

In 1903, to increase the intensity of the light, a fourth order lens replaced the fifth order lens. The following year the new fog signal went into operation.

The great Earthquake of 1906 did relatively little damage to the keepers' dwellings considering the magnitude. It did cause the chimneys to collapse, and the bridge between the bluff and the fort was displaced enough to make it too dangerous to use. Although the Fort itself sustained some damage, the little iron lighthouse came through unscathed.

During the years between 1933, and 1937, Fort Point, was used as the base of operations for the construction of the Golden Gate Bridge, with drafters setting up shop in the old barracks. A cafeteria came to life in the second tier gun rooms. Artisans swarmed over the site as the great anchorages were set, and the span of the bridge rose.

The Golden Gate Bridge spelled the end of the lighthouse at Fort Point. The arch within the bridge, designed to protect the fort for future generations, also obstructed the light from mariners. September 1934, saw the lighthouse deactivated. Mounted on the bridge anchorage north of the fort, an automated light and fog signal went into operation.

The military occupied the fort again for the duration of World War II. Placed atop the fort were 100 soldiers on submarine watch, operating searchlights, and rapid-fire cannons. To prevent Japanese submarines from entering the bay, huge steel nets were set in place under the Golden Gate Bridge. The nets, strung underwater from the Marina Green to Sausalito were supported by dozens of buoys and opened by Navy tugs when allied ships needed to enter the bay.

Fort Point keepers dwellings (note the bridge to the tower across the chasm)
Photo courtesy of the United States Lighthouse Society

LIME POINT

Lime Point
Photo courtesy of The United States Lighthouse Society

Lime Point, along with Angel Island's Point Knox, Humboldt Harbour, Point Montara, and Año Nuevo Island, all began life as fog signal stations, to combat California's greatest maritime threat-fog. All five would eventually add lights to their stations, but the fog signal had been the impetus for their construction. Between Cape Mendocino in the north and Point Sur, south of Monterey, there is but one spot that the fog penetrates the coastal mountains of California, the San Francisco Bay. Positioned at Lime Point, the fog can be seen as it pours into the Golden Gate from the ocean on an average of 106 days a year.

Lime Point, the shining example and largest of the great fog signals, is located underneath the northern end of the Golden Gate Bridge. The station included a huge brick two-story keepers' structure, a boiler shed, a woodshed, a coal house and a 1500-foot tramway that ran from the station to Lime Point Cove. Two huge boilers supplied the steam for the enormous twin whistles mounted atop the fog signal building. The piercing whistles could clearly be heard in the North Beach community of San Francisco across the bay.

The station's water supply was fed by a single spring in Lime Point Cove. This proved inadequate, so it was supplemented by a second spring in order to provide a sufficient supply for the station. In total, four water tanks stored the water needed to operate the station.

On September 10, 1883, Lime Point fog signal roared to life. In the first year of operation a large landslide occurred from Lime Point Bluff, (now the location of the base of the Golden Gate Bridge) damaging the water tank so badly that it had to be drained, removed, and rebuilt. Landslides of this type were a common occurrence at Lime Point. Slides repeatedly destroyed the trail to the station and created varying degrees of damage over the years.

Point Montara and Angel Island's Point Knox each joined Lime Point on November 26, 1900, in exhibiting identical 300mm lights for the first time. The light at Lime Point was mounted on the side of the fog signal building only 19-feet above the water.

In 1903, Lime Point became the focus of a new experiment. The use of crude petroleum to power the boilers feeding the steam whistles. The fog signal had an excessively long blast using a tremendous amount of steam. When use converted from coal to oil, cost dropped almost 75 percent. The experiment was such a success that the following year a tank and a fill pipe were installed to pump oil directly from a barge into the fuel tank.

In 1923, an automated secondary light and siren installed at Point Diablo went into service. About the size of a large outhouse, the station is located halfway between Point Bonita and Lime Point, and remains active today. It was the responsibility of the keepers of Lime Point to maintain the small light. Between the two stations is a distance of about one and a half miles. A cable and a special telephone were installed for communication between the stations. This allowed them to monitor the siren remotely between the weekly scheduled maintenance.

On January 5, 1933, construction of the Golden Gate Bridge began. Toward the end of construction, the station and many other things suddenly began to take on a new color; orange vermilion, the color of the bridge. Having just painted the entire fog station white, the constant overspray from the men painting above tinted not only the laundry hung out to dry but also the entire station.

On May 27, 1937, the bridge opened to pedestrians for one day. The following day one of California's greatest architectural marvels opened to vehicular traffic. The opening of the bridge seemed to create a new problem for the crew stationed at Lime Point, when some people delighted in throwing their bottles and trash from the bridge. A bottle dropped from a height of 740-feet is a potentially life threatening situation. Keepers needed to keep an eye on the sky while performing their usual duties. With the completion of the bridge, travel into San Francisco was much easier for the keepers and their families.

In June 1960, the Pacific Far East Lines *India Bear* struck Lime Point during a heavy fog. The ship severed the air pipes to the siren as it hit, and destroyed the station bathroom before coming to rest on the reef. The ship had miraculously missed the keepers' dwelling by mere feet.

Fallen from grace, the Lime Point Fog Signal Station is but a shadow of its former self. The closest view of the structure is from the walkway on the northern side of the Golden Gate Bridge, or the parking lot of the visitor's center. Below the bridge, the lighthouse has been fenced, barricaded, and closed off to all visitors. There is no decent view of Lime Point Light Station to be found from anywhere underneath the bridge. Except for the fog signal building itself, nothing else remains of the once proud station that stands alone on an outcropping just 20-feet wide and 100-feet long.

Lime Point after being struck by the India Bear
Photo courtesy of The United States Lighthouse Society

MILE ROCK

One of California's most unique lighthouses, an architectural and engineering feat is unfortunately lost forever. Deactivated in 1969, and subsequently removed, all that remains of Mile Rock is the caisson, topped with a helicopter pad outfitted with a beacon. The caisson is visible from Point Bonita and the Golden Gate Bridge, but the closest viewing spot to the actual location can be found at land's end at Lincoln Park. Lighthouse fans will find this vantage point is unequaled in California. From this spot you can see Mile Rock light, Point Bonita, Point Diablo secondary light, Lime Point, and Fort Point.

Located a mile outside the Golden Gate Bridge, and measuring only 30-feet by 40-feet, Mile Rock rises 20-feet above the water. Just a short distance away is Little Mile Rock. The two rocks were often covered by waves or hidden by fog, posing a navigational hazard for many years. The Lighthouse Service anchored a bell buoy near Mile Rock in November of 1889. The buoy was often submerged in the strong currents surrounding the rocks and proved to be inadequate for the job. The surrounding underwater area was home to reefs, rocks, and land shelves lying just below the water, posing a threat to navigation.

The *SS City of Rio De Janeiro* was a 344-foot long, iron-hulled vessel originally built for hauling cargo and passengers between Brazil and the United States. When the venture proved unprofitable, the ship sold to the Pacific Mail Steamship Company. The company's new route was between San Francisco and Hong Kong. The crew was made up of 84 Chinese men, while the officers were all American. Two Chinese members of the crew spoke both Chinese and English and acted as the translators when hand signals were not adequate. This would prove to be a fatal mistake. At a time when communication was the most important thing for survival, there was none.

In January 1901, the *SS City of Rio De Janeiro* was making her 80th crossing. Loaded with passengers, and a cargo of silk, rice, and tea, the *Rio* set sail for San Francisco.

The crossing was difficult. Rough seas had made many of the passengers sick and they were resting in their cabins. The *Rio* was two days behind schedule when the ship finally sighted the Marin Headlands. As they approached, a heavy fog enveloped the ship. Captain William Ward gave order to drop anchor; they would have to sit out the fog.

Frederick "Little" Jordan, the local pilot, arrived that evening and boarded the vessel. Jordan had 11 years experience and was known for his skill and abilities navigating the narrow channel into the Golden Gate. In the morning when the fog began to lift, the Captain ordered the ship underway, but they would never reach the San Francisco docks.

Suddenly a heavy fog shrouded the *Rio*, and within minutes visibility had decreased so much that from one end of the ship, you could not see the opposite end of the vessel. A heavy ebb tide was running and unbeknownst to them, they were drifting starboard toward the rocks on the southern side of the channel. The ship ran aground somewhere close to Fort Point. The captain ordered an evacuation, which began smoothly but quickly went terribly wrong. The lack of communication between officers and crew was

Mile Rock
Photo courtesy of The United States Lighthouse Society

crippling. Most of the passengers were asleep when the ship hit and many did not want to leave their staterooms until it was too late. Some refused to believe they were in grave danger, while others were hopeful of saving their valuables. Within ten to 20 minutes, the ship broke free from the rocks and quickly sank. Bonita Cove Lifeboat Station was not even aware of the shipwreck for two hours, and by that time, many of the bodies had swept out to sea.

The *Rio* carried 11 lifeboats, and only three were lowered during the disaster, and two of those were lost. As with most shipwrecks, accounts vary, but between 81-84 survived out of the 209-235 people on the ship. The intact wreck lies in 320-feet of water just off the Golden Gate near Point Diablo.

The shipwrecks resulting U.S. Supreme Court Case
O'HARA v. LUCKENBACH SS CO.
Argued Nov. 19, 1925.
Decided Jan. 4, 1926.

> "Act... provides that not less than 75 per centum of the crew in each department shall be able to understand any order given by the officers of such vessel." …"Like that of the *SS City of Rio De Janeiro* …which sank with many of its lifeboats un-launched because the crew of Chinese sailors was unable to understand the language in which the orders were given."

In 1902, the Secretary of the Treasury decided on the establishment of a light and fog-signal on the larger one of the two Mile Rocks in San Francisco Bay.

The winning contract for building the Lighthouse on Mile Rock went to James A. McMahon. In 1904, McMahon took a group of able-bodied construction workers to the site for the first time. Upon seeing the wave washed Mile Rock and the dangerous conditions in which they were expected to work, the men quit. McMahon then gathered sailors for the job, who were more familiar with the hazardous conditions of the sea than with construction. The treacherous waters surrounding the rock often sent men tumbling off the rock and into the sea, limiting the work schedule to times of low tide. The arduous task of raising the caisson went slow. The four-foot thick concrete walls proved difficult to erect, but upon completion of the caisson, work progressed at a faster pace. The lighthouse was a white, three-tiered steel tower erected upon a black caisson, capped with a black lantern room. A third order Fresnel lens provided the light for Mile Rock. Shortly after completion, the 1906 earthquake occurred, but the lighthouse survived with no damage.

Life on the rock was lonely and isolated. Families, prohibited on this dangerous lighthouse, lived on shore. Wives were known to stand on land's end near Point Lobos, using lights to say good night to their men.

As was the case on lightships, the men would dread the days of fog when the diaphone fog signal fired up. Nowhere could one escape the booming blast of the horn. The blast was relentless, sounding every 15 seconds, sometimes with fog that could last for days.

On May 18, 1915, a unique occasion took place on the Mile Rock Lighthouse. An event that would have been out of place at most lighthouses, but Mile Rock made the occurrence stand out all the more. Eighteen-year-old Gaynel Dresser of San Francisco decided that she wanted to add a kick to her wedding to Cyril J. MacMeekin of San Jose, by having it performed on Mile Rock. The happy couple and their four guests climbed the Jacob's ladder up to the boom and proceeded to the turret where the ceremony

Mile Rock
Photo courtesy of The United States Lighthouse Society

took place.

The Coast Guard tried to automate the lighthouse twice in the early sixties. An armored steel electrical cable was run underwater from the lighthouse to the mainland. Both times the cable was moved by the strong currents in the bay, and severed while being dragged across the rocks. The entire lighthouse, removed in August 1966, gave way to a helicopter pad installed on the caisson. Generators provided the necessary electricity for the beacon and fog signal for many years, but has been replaced with a solar array to provide power. The Fresnel lens resides in the Old Point Loma Lighthouse, in San Diego's Cabrillo National Park.

MILE ROCK LIGHT-HOUSE, SAN FRANCISCO HARBOR, CAL.

Mile Rock Diagram
Photo courtesy of The United States Lighthouse Society

POINT BONITA

Spending weeks at sea with no sight of earth, can make a man yearn for dry land. Upon a sailor's return home the first sign that they had reached their destination, was the shining beacon of a lighthouse. The first visible light for the seaman approaching San Francisco was also the most dramatic. Point Bonita, situated at the northwestern point of the Marin headlands, rests on basalt outcroppings at the entrance to the San Francisco Bay, just two miles west of the Golden Gate Bridge. Part of one of the largest urban national parks in the world, the Golden Gate National Recreation Area also includes Alcatraz Island and Fort Point. It is just a short drive from the Golden Gate Bridge to the lighthouse, on a steep and windy headland road. Such a remote and isolated location makes it hard to imagine being only seven miles from the hustle and bustle of San Francisco. History buffs will find the area rich with artifacts from California's early days. The Marin Headlands were the first defense on the northern side of the bay, against invaders from the sea. Gun turrets and batteries dot the hillsides in even greater numbers than on San Francisco's southern entrance.

The lighthouse is reached via a half-mile trail that takes you past the remains of the lifesaving station and through a man-made tunnel drilled through the mountain. Huge iron doors cover the tunnel except during the minimal hours of operation, effectively removing access to the lighthouse. On the other side of the tunnel, a suspension bridge spans a chasm to reach a small outcropping of land where the lighthouse resides.

In March 1853, the *Tennessee* wrecked two and a half miles from Point Bonita. That same year, the *San Francisco* ran aground near Point Bonita, prompting the Lighthouse Board to build the third of San Francisco's lighthouses.

On April 30, 1855, the first Point Bonita Lighthouse began its service. It was built using the same Cape Cod style as the other six original lighthouses in the state. A lonely and isolated spot, Point Bonita had no direct communications with the rest of the world and no inhabitants within five miles. Sausalito was seven miles away, but the station had only a horse and cart to get to town. In the first nine months the light would see seven different light-keepers.

In August of 1855, a cannon transferred to Point Bonita from the Benicia Arsenal became California's first fog signal. The cannon, a 24 pounder siege gun, required firing every half hour during periods of heavy fog. The cannon was eventually discontinued due to the overwhelming cost of gunpowder, and replaced with a 1,500 pound bell.

In the early 1870s, the Lighthouse Board made the decision to relocate the light to the western extremity of land's end. An incline railway built to bring materials from the ships to the construction site of the new

Point Bonita Lighthouse
Photo courtesy of The United States Lighthouse Society

lighthouse went into use, and a tunnel drilled through the rocks created a new entrance to the Point Bonita Lighthouse. On February 1, 1877, the second lighthouse at Point Bonita began its operation.

A 20-foot long, first class, coal-powered, steam fog signal went into operation on the eastern most side of land's end. A water reservoir and windmill were installed to pump the water to the fog signal building.

In an interview given 86 years after leaving Point Bonita, Agnes Johanna Frey, daughter of Niles Frey, assistant light-keeper at Point Bonita, spoke of the isolation especially felt by her mother. She remembered how her mother threw a batch of kneaded dough out the window to the rocks below, out of frustration over trying to learn how to bake bread. Only afterwards did she discover that her wedding ring had come off in the dough, and now resided on the cliffs below. Niles climbed down the cliff, found the dough, and retrieved the ring for his bride.

Agnes dealt with the isolation as well, at this time in history there were no children at the lighthouse for Agnes to play with. All that would change a few years later when children graced the point with their ever-bounding curiosity. As recounted in her book "Three Beams of Light," Norma Engel spoke of growing up at the point during the 1906 earthquake, watching across the bay as the fires raged through San Francisco.

The great earthquake of 1906 toppled chimneys, cracked foundations, and destroyed the assistant keeper's quarters. The Engel family of four found themselves displaced from their home. Out of necessity the family found themselves living in the one-room fog-signal building, abandoned three years earlier. The other keepers, their families, and the men from the lifesaving station, helped the family through the tough times, bringing them food and helping them restore an old wood stove that was discarded before the quake. After a long two years of waiting and living in the fog-signal building, construction of the new quarters was finally finished.

In January 1915, the *Eureka*, carrying two tons of dynamite, ran aground on the rocks below the lighthouse. The first assistant Alexander Martin attempted to rescue the men by dropping a rope down the cliff, and lowering himself down. As Martin reached the end of the rope, he found himself 50-feet short of the ground. Martin had to climb back up the rope and run to the lifesaving station for help. He and the crew managed to save everyone but the first mate of the ship.

In 1926, electricity came to Point Bonita, followed by a radio beacon in 1938. The land bridge to the lighthouse was eroded by a landslide in 1944, so a temporary wooden bridge was built to take its place. The temporary fix lasted for ten years, when it was replaced with a new suspension bridge.

On April 2, 1981, the United States Coast Guard decommissioned Point Bonita Light Station, leaving automation to control the point. The light station began a new life in September of 1984, when the National Park Service opened Point Bonita on a very restricted schedule to the public.

FARALLON ISLAND

Thirty miles west of the Golden Gate, a small cluster of islands break the surface of the water. Obscured by rolling banks of fog during the summer months, the Farallon Islands presented a major navigational hazard for early voyagers. The islands are part of quartz diorite batholiths extending 12 miles in length and one and a half miles in breadth at its widest point. Running parallel to the Gulf of Farallones is the Continental Shelf, where ocean depths drop from 50-60-feet around the islands to more than 1000-feet deep.

The Farallon Islands extend over an area of seven miles. Southeast Farallon is actually two small islets drawn together by a 300-foot tall ridge of rocks that make one contiguous island. Southeast Farallon is the only one of the islands ever inhabited, and its highest peak is home to the 41-foot tall lighthouse. Two and a half miles away, Middle Farallon is simply a rock 50-to-60-feet in diameter protruding from the ocean, reaching 20-30-feet out of the water. North Farallon is actually 12 rocks that pierce the ocean surface in three groupings. The rock with the greatest height is 160-feet high, while the southernmost rock stands only 20-feet above the water. Below the surface, the rocks pose much greater danger.

The islands have had extremely limited access since 1969. Restricted only to Point Reyes Bird Observatory (PRBO) scientists, who have provided a year-round stewardship to the wildlife on these islands. A cooperative agreement with the U.S. Fish and Wildlife Service has produced the longest data set on seabirds and marine mammals in North America.

Sir Francis Drake, the first recorded visitor to the islands, named them the "Islands of Saint James." Upon his arrival in 1579, Drake stopped to replenish his food stores with the abundant supply of birds and seals.

Once again, the history of California turns with the gold rush. As the population of San Francisco grew, so did its need for food. One of the mainstays of everyone's diet was chicken eggs, but in California in 1850, chickens were rare and very expensive.

To fill the void, millions of Murre eggs, removed from the cliff ledges on Southeast Farallon Island were sold in San Francisco. The Murre colonies on the Farallones were quite possibly the largest in the United States at one time, but would be devastated after decades of picking by the egg companies. Conflicting claims over ownership, occupancy, and the right to collect eggs from Southeast Farallon took place between groups of fishermen, egg company agents, light-keepers, and government representatives, and would continue for the next 40 years.

Southeast Farallon Island was chosen by the Lighthouse Board to be one of the first seven lighthouse locations in California. The lighthouse would be located on the peak of Beacon Rock, 354-feet above sea level.

The 1850s were a turbulent time on Southeast Farallon; anyone who could supply eggs to the city could make a fortune. Companies were formed around the collecting of eggs found on the Farallones. It was the Pacific Egg Company (also known as the Farallon Egg Company) formed in 1855, that laid claim to Southeast Farallon. The Italian fishing community was particularly opposed to their monopoly. Other egg companies tried their hand at picking eggs from the Northern Farallones, but it was much more treacherous.

When the Lighthouse Tender, *Oriole* arrived with the construction crew and supplies needed to begin work on the lighthouse, the armed egg pickers refused to allow the ship to land. The egg pickers wanted nothing to do with a lighthouse on the island. They did not want a flashing light frightening the birds and ruining their lucrative venture. The construction workers were there to build a lighthouse, not fight a war, so the ship retreated and returned to San Francisco. At the request of the Lighthouse Service, a Coast Survey steamer crewed by well-armed United States seamen was sent to retake Southeast Farallon Island. Presented with a different set of circumstances, the egg pickers reevaluated the situation and decided a lighthouse was just what the island needed.

Southeast Farallon Island
Photo courtesy of The United States Lighthouse Society

When work finally began, the laborers soon tired of hauling the materials up to the peak over the sharp treacherous rocks. Each man could only carry four or five bricks at a time, so the men staged a sit down strike and demanded a mule. Their strike affected the desired result and soon a mule named Jerry arrived, although dreadfully seasick.

Quarried on the site, the stone used to build the tower underwent additional fortification, as stonemasons internally lined the stone with bricks.

The French ship *St. Joseph* arrived in San Francisco in December 1854, carrying the first order lens intended for the lighthouse on Southeast Farallon. The lens was transported to the island with a crew of men to carry the pieces up the peak to the tower. When the men began assembling the Fresnel, to everyone's surprise, they discovered that the lens was too big for the cupola, and would not fit. Therefore, in December of 1854, the 41-foot tower came down, and a new lighthouse was constructed to accommodate the first order lens. Standing 12-feet high and eight-feet in diameter, the lens was six-inches thick and had eight sides. On January 1, 1855, the lighthouse on Southeast Farallon Island beamed its light over the surrounding ocean for the first time.

The season for egging on the Farallones was roughly from mid May until the end of July. During this time a crew of 15-20 men, living in crude shanties near the landing dock, would collect eggs and prepare them for shipping. The process of picking was to clear an area of the island of eggs. If they could not clear an area for a day or two they would throw the eggs into the ocean, so they could begin again fresh. The Murre is about half the size of a duck and lays an egg the size of a goose egg. It is a thick shelled egg, a little larger than the average chicken egg, but it spoils faster, giving the egg an undesirable fishy taste after two or three days. The Murre will normally lay two brown or greenish speckled eggs, but when robbed it increases its output to six or even eight eggs. The eggs were quite popular in San Francisco, where restaurants and bakers used the eggs for omelets, cakes, and custards.

The pickers wore baggy shirts constructed from flour sacks with holes cut for their head and arms. The sack was then tied tightly around their waist. The men deposited the eggs inside through a slit in the front. The shoes worn by the men had soles constructed of rope, not leather. This gave them a greater grip on the wet, uneven rocks as they climbed the slopes. The men could carry 18-to-20-dozen eggs in any one trip. They also carried guns, to keep the competing companies at a distance, because ugly brawls were known to break out between rivals.

Captain Dagget was the owner of the sailing ship *Lucas,* a passenger ship that left Victoria, British Columbia in October 1858, with more than 175 disillusioned gold seekers from the Frasier River. In the middle of the night, after days in a heavy fog, the *Lucas* struck Seal Rock, about 300-yards southeast of the main island. The ship sank in less than an hour leaving the passengers to swim toward the island. Ropes thrown into the surf helped people pull themselves through the water to the beach. Light-keepers helped in the rescue and provided comfort to the passengers while waiting for a rescue ship to arrive. The United States Steamer *Active,* under the command of Captain Alden, performed the rescue, transporting all hands to San Francisco. The vessel and cargo were a total loss, and 15-30 people lost their lives.

Prompted by the sinking of the *Lucas* in 1858, Major Hartman Bache, the great grandson of Benjamin Franklin and engineer for the twelfth district, devised a fog signal consisting of a huge trumpet, six-inches in diameter at its smaller end, mounted over a natural blowhole. When incoming waves forced air up through the passage, the trumpet would sound, and was audible seven or eight miles away. Unfortunately, it was mostly silent during calm weather, such as foggy days. During heavy surf and for the duration of storms the horn would roar to life.

In June 1859, Inspector De Camp of the twelfth district in San Francisco complained to Washington about Egg Company men trespassing on Southeast Farallon. The egg pickers had built shanties, and claimed the island as their own. In May of 1860, the egg pickers ordered the government keepers to leave the island at gunpoint. C. S. Boggs, another inspector for the Twelfth District, reported that in July, one of the assistant keepers was assaulted.

Federal authorities arrested four armed fishermen on Southeast Farallon Island in April 1863, who had occupied the island and obstructed light-keepers in the performance of their duty. In May 1863, armed crews under the command of Lieutenant Commander C. M. Scammon landed on the beach in three small boats. They made their way to the house occupied by D. F. Bachelder and 30 men, and ordered the men off the island.

In June 1863, a crew of seven armed fishermen departed from a San Francisco dock, heading for the Farallones. They were spotted by egg company employees and reported to Lieutenant Commander Scammon. The next day the *Shubrick* made its way toward the island where it found two boats and a schooner off shore. Scammon took the word of the men when they told him they planned to fish North Farallon, and returned to San Francisco. The egg gatherers on Southeast Farallon, aware of their presence, feared an attack. Early one June morning, one of the boats, with

25 armed men aboard, approached the shore with the intent to dispossess the 15 pickers from harvesting Murre eggs. The Egg Company foreman and five of his men tried to warn off the boat, but the fisherman began shooting. Edward Perkins, an American on shore was shot in the stomach, and died a few minutes later. Arrested were Bachelder and five of his men, in connection with the murder of Edward Perkins. A few days later, murder charges were dropped against all but two men, who faced the reduced rate of manslaughter.

After the infighting between rival egg pickers, the Pacific Egg Company began to buy the rights of other companies. The Pacific Egg Company continued to collect eggs on Southeast Farallon Island after the "Egg War" was over. As the years went by, they continued to become more stubborn and demanding over their claims to the island. In 1871, the government became so disgusted with the whole situation that the Lighthouse Board decided that it would revoke any authority to fish or land on Southeast Farallon. The number of eggs harvested continued to drop; from 1872 to 1873 egg collection dropped almost 28 thousand dozen.

In 1875, the United States Attorney General informed the California Attorney General that he was to protect the light-keepers on Farallon Island from offense or injury by any egg company or sealing operation. In 1876, the Lighthouse Board served the Egg Company notice that they could no longer trespass on the Lighthouse Reservation. A report from the Engineer Secretary stated that the Lighthouse Board felt the Egg Company had no true title to the island that they were now and had always been, trespassers. To exacerbate the situation, while first assistant Louis Engelbrecht was collecting eggs one day, he fell and broke both legs.

The Pacific Egg Company nevertheless was still collecting eggs on the island in 1880. They leased the privilege of capturing seals to another company, which began killing seals defiantly against the laws of the United States, and to the annoyance of the keepers. The company and its pickers had become so arrogant that it began to deny the keepers the right to collect eggs. The light-keeper at the time, Hess, complained to the inspector that the pickers had found him days earlier with his shirt filled with eggs and had knocked him over and rolled him down the rocks, breaking the eggs and humiliating him.

Now considered detrimental to the health of the light-keepers, the continued presence of the Egg Company was no longer tolerable. In the interest of navigation, all trespassers had to leave the island, and from then on, permission to land on the island required approval of the District Superintendent of Lighthouses. For 26 years, the Pacific Egg Company had claimed exclusive control of the island and its wildlife, but in May of

1881, its control fell. The government steamer, *Manzanita* arrived with the United States Marshall, an officer, and 20 soldiers to remove the pickers from the island. Removed without incident, were 11 egg pickers, who were transported to San Francisco with their belongings.

The Pacific Egg Company filed suit for damages against the United States District Attorney claiming unlawful eviction from the premises. The company claimed the island as its own, declaring rights, title, and physical possession for over 25 years. After four years, the case was dismissed from the circuit court at the plaintiffs' cost.

Collecting by the keepers continued, and they continued shipping eggs to San Francisco throughout the 1880s. As egg numbers steadily decreased, so did the Murre population. Leverett M. Loomis of the California Academy of Sciences sought to ban any further egg collecting on the islands and contacted William Dutcher, the chairman of the American Ornithologists' Union's Bird-Protection Committee in New York to help. He sought to prevent the extermination of the Farallon population of murres, gulls, and petrels. In a letter to the secretary of the Lighthouse Board, Dutcher claimed that by allowing the keepers to harvest eggs it went beyond their duty as a public servant and created a commercial venture on government property. The Lighthouse Board agreed, and in December 1896, they prohibited the light-keepers from any form of wild bird egg collecting for sale. Light-keepers continued to collect gull eggs for themselves on the west end of the island well into the new century, but the trade of selling bird eggs from the Farallones had come to an end.

At some point during the island's history, someone introduced Belgian hares to the island, and they had multiplied spectacularly; the rabbits survived on the sparse vegetation in among the rocks. During the rainy season, the rabbits were fat with white meat that was sweet and succulent, but during the dry season when vegetation was sparse, they became stringy and unfit to eat. Rabbit was a welcome addition to the residents' usual diet of fresh fish and eggs. The families raised other livestock on the island as well, goats, turkeys, and chickens also added to the food supply.

The Lighthouse Service occupied about a dozen buildings, and usually the island had no more than 18 residents. The only connection with the outside world was when the supply ship would arrive. During the winter months the boat would be unable to land for weeks at a time. A Farallon light-keeper led a lonely monotonous existence, in an inhospitable place, another world away. The vision that was San Francisco lay right before their eyes, so close and yet so far.

Life for a light-keeper was a hard existence; the climb to the tower itself was a grueling task in heavy weather. Even in fine weather the climb was steep and rocky. The trail was a series of switchbacks with no railing. The light-keepers took this trail day and night, rain or shine, every single day. At times weather could be so severe that the light-keeper had to make the trek on hands and knees so as not to be blown off the mountain.

Sometimes the Italian fisherman would come by and leave fresh fish and wine, thankful for the protection of the light. "Boat day" on the island was a major event. Grain for the horse (Patty) and mule (Jerry) would be on board as well as tons of coal for the steam siren and all of the necessary station supplies. A small railroad built on the island, laid over gullies, crevasses, and rocks ran from the dock to the dwellings and to the fog signal. A flatcar pulled by Jerry or Patty transported the supplies, primarily coal for the fog signal and oil for the light from the dock to their ultimate destination. The only way to get the fuel for the lamp to the lighthouse was to pack it up the hill, the oil barrels strapped to each side of one of the animals. It was not long before Jerry came to recognize the blast of the *Madrono's* whistle and he would run and hide when the ship arrived. Light-keepers could spend the better part of the day trying to hunt Jerry down. The island population held Jerry, the oldest inhabitant of the island, in esteem. He seemed to sense the change of weather, and would get very excited. Jerry would sit and snort, as he peered off into the direction of a

Farallon Island Lighthouse
Photo courtesy of The United States Lighthouse Society

coming storm up to 24 hours before it arrived. He loved to play with the children, even letting them pull his tail and gather around his legs without kicking. Also known to steal cookies and cakes left out on the window sill to cool, Jerry was never able to resist the sweets.

For a child on the island, life was a game - places to play, things to explore and animals and birds to examine. During the Christmas season, the *Madrono* would arrive with a tree and presents, and on the big day light-keeper Beeman would play Santa. The final day for Jerry came on Christmas day 1873; Jerry had been sick for about ten days and finally succumbed to old age. The old mule had been on the island since 1854. He was buried the next day and missed by all.

Life for families on the island was hard and dangerous. With no doctor present, illness or accident could mean disaster. While on Farallon, the O'Caine family lost three of their children. Two died from diphtheria, and one fell from the landing and drowned. The Beeman's lost a son after a desperate effort to row 27 miles in an open boat to the mainland for help. The Lighthouse Board attempted to improve communication and transportation to the island.

The turn of the century brought the telephone to the island via an amazing 18 mile-long, undersea cable laid from Point Reyes to the Farallon Islands. It allowed direct, instant communication between the island and the mainland. In 1903, the cable broke and the Point Reyes lifesaving crew was called to grapple for the cable. The cable was recovered with help from the crew of the steamer *Alexander Volta* who also helped in splicing it and restoring communication to the island.

The Farallon Islands were essentially unaffected by the great quake of 1906. In fact, the only communication coming out of the San Francisco Bay Area, was relayed from the *USS Chicago,* anchored in San Francisco Bay, to the Farallon Islands. The communiqué was then sent to Point Arguello and placed onto land lines. The Farallon Naval radio station was also the first to communicate with the Hawaiian Islands in the fall of 1908.

The islands became part of the Farallon Reservation on February 27, 1909, when Theodore Roosevelt signed it into law. The reservation did not include Southeast Farallon. The island came under the jurisdiction of the Lighthouse Service, who protected the island as a preserve and breeding ground for 12 species of native birds.

Getting onto the island itself always presented safety issues, and several different methods of hoisting people onto the island went through tests. The secret to not spinning in each contraption contrived was in the passengers' weight distribution. A wooden ship's chair was used for a time. A box like configuration was a popular method, since the passenger had no way to fall off. A canvas basket used latter by the USCG had the same effect. All these methods were eventually replaced with the Billy Pugh personnel net, a safer transfer device still in use today that allowed personnel to embark and disembark quickly and safely. Unfortunately, none of the early methods was completely safe. A small boat could roll, or someone could fall from a basket or line, or be swamped by a rogue wave and dumped into the sea.

The first commercial radio broadcast had taken place in 1922, and by the mid 1920s most of the families on the island had a radio and reception was good. The inhabitants were lucky that one of the keepers had a wife with a nursing background. Louise Johnson could at least help with any medical crisis until a doctor could arrive.

Thomas Atkinson had been stationed at St. George Reef Lighthouse, where families were not allowed. When he transferred from the lonely isolated North Seal Rock, to the Farallon Lighthouse, he was joined by his wife. It was not to anyone's surprise that the couple was soon expecting a child. They were surprised, when the baby decided to arrive eight weeks earlier than expected. When Mrs. Atkinson went into labor, radio messages sent out a plea requesting a doctor. Until he arrived, Louise Johnson had to take charge. On February 19, 1927, Delpha Atkinson became the only child to be born on the Farallon Islands in the 20th century. The only other child born on the island had been Farallone O'caine in the 1890s, daughter of Mrs. Cyrus O'caine. Louise Johnson delivered the baby before the doctor arrived. When he did get there, seasick from the voyage, he charged the Atkinson's $50 for the trouble and spent the day fishing. When a Navy man was fatally burned in a fire, the Navy stationed a pharmacist's mate on the island, so they could provide a greater range of medical supplies.

The Great Depression hit America hard, but areas existed that were not directly affected, like the population on Southeast Farallon Island. Housing was paid for, there were plenty of food supplies, and the keepers were gainfully employed. The keepers enjoyed having parties where they would play bridge or dance to the music on the radio. The residents used the huge cement rain catchment basin as a tennis court in good weather. Fishing was a continual pastime on the island, providing relaxation and food. Some would hold Sunday religious services, complete with bible readings.

During World War I, 20 marines under the command of a sergeant patrolled the island. In October 1922, after continual damage of equipment and fixtures by the rabbit population, 50 Navy men were brought to the island armed with clubs to exterminate the bunnies. During gale force winds, the men chased hares all over the rocky slopes in a ridiculous and unsuccessful effort to rid the island of the rabbits.

The Lighthouse Service had always been a civilian organization, so when the military took over in 1939, life for the family-oriented service began to change. The focus would now be more of a short-term assignment rather than a long-term residency. The Coast Guard did nothing to change the conditions of the operation on the island, but they did enforce strict conservation to protect the birds and marine life.

The largest population the island ever had came during World War II. In 1944 the liberty ship *Henry Bergh* ran directly into Southeast Farallon Island. The *Henry Bergh was* filled to more than twice its capacity with a crew of 100, and 1300 sailors on their way home to San Francisco from Pearl Harbor. The ship, enveloped in a thick fog for more than 36 hours, had been host to a large party that had lasted into the wee hours of the morning. The captain, Joseph C. Chambers, erroneous in his calculations of wind and currents was almost ten miles off course. The loud party prevented the passengers or crew from hearing the fog signal as it bellowed from the quickly approaching island. Just before five, a faint whistle heard onboard, was immediately followed by the first glimpse of the rocks. The ship ran aground about 200-yards offshore of Southeast Farallon Island while running full speed at 11-knots. It had been too late for evasive action, and the attempts made to back away were futile. An SOS sent from the *Henry Bergh* and received in San Francisco saw rescue teams dispatched, but the first vessel would not make it to the island for three hours. The abandonment of the ship was a very orderly affair. Some of the men made their way through the cold water to the island, via a breeches buoy set up between the island rocks and the ship. Eight lifeboats brought men to the beach 25 at a time, until the rescue boats arrived from San Francisco. No lives were lost in the event, and the ship was thoroughly evacuated by afternoon. The ship would only last for a matter of days before it broke into pieces and sank. The Captain was found to be at fault for allowing the party noise to be so loud as to drown out the fog signal. For his failure to take soundings, and the errors he made in plotting the course, the captain was demoted to the rank of first mate.

Women and children were removed from the island in 1965, to reduce costs associated with medical and other emergencies, such as shipping and helicopter use.

The Farallon Islands came under protection as a National Wildlife Refuge in 1969. A new automated beacon replaced the original Fresnel lens in 1972, which stands on display at the visitor center in the Argonaut Hotel across from the Hyde Street Pier in San Francisco.

Very few living individuals have ever stepped foot on the Farallon

Islands, and for the protection of the island and its varied species, very few ever will. In addition to the official restrictions in place, the natural restrictions are just as harsh. There is no natural harbor, the waters around the island are very rough, and there is nowhere to disembark safely.

Without human interaction, the island, teams with life once more. Farallon Island provides a critical habitat for the largest concentration of breeding seabirds within the contiguous United States, The Gulf of the Farallones National Marine Sanctuary is one of the richest ecosystems on the planet. Species found within the sanctuary include, Leatherback Sea Turtles, Marbled Murrelets, Northern Elephant Seals, Northern Fur Seals, California and Steller Sea Lions, Gray Whales, Humpbacks, and Orcas. The Farallones play host to one of the planets few Blue Whale populations. Other species found are the Pacific White-sided Dolphin, and more than a quarter million breeding seabirds. Rockfish and the Tufted Puffin also call the Farallones home.

Farallon Light Station
Photo courtesy of The United States Lighthouse Society

Circular No. 8, of 1895,

Office of U.S. Light-House Inspector,

Twelfth District,

San Francisco, Cal., 25 April, 1895.

At all stations the Journal is to be written up daily by the Keeper and kept in the most convenient place, accessible at <u>all</u> times to <u>all</u> the assistants.

Assistants are expected and required to review it repeatedly, and to call the attention of the Keeper to any oversights or inaccuracies.

Keepers will acknowledge receipt of this circular, stating also whether or not it has been posted as ordered by Circular No. 7, of 1895.

Henry E. Nichols,

Commander, U.S.N.,

Inspector 12th Light-House District.

California Circular - 1895
Photo courtesy of The United States Lighthouse Society

Lighting the North

POINT REYES

Point Reyes Lighthouse
Photo courtesy of The United States Lighthouse Society

Point Reyes is an odd shaped peninsula that juts out ten miles into the Pacific creating a dangerous headland with rocky cliffs. Located 35 miles northwest of San Francisco, this national treasure is much the same as it has been for decades. Nature's diversity covers the cape, from forest areas filled with thick brush, to rolling hills covered with grass, surrounded by beaches. Dairy farms dating back for generations dot the countryside.

Isolated and rugged, Point Reyes remained relatively unaffected by the gold rush. The point did gain fame as a deadly, jutting snag that threatened every ship approaching the Golden Gate from the north. When California gained statehood in 1850, the dangers of its rocky shores were not well known. Conditions at Point Reyes can be extreme. Fog here is some of the thickest found at any lighthouse in the United States, sometimes logging up to 2,700 hours of fog a year. Wind gusts can occur in excess of 100 miles per hour, and winds clocked as high as 133 miles per hour have hit this point.

In August 1854, Congress made appropriations to build a light station at Point Reyes. In September, a new map of the coast of California showed Point Reyes reserved "for lighthouse purposes." Unfortunately, in 1854, the United States did not yet have title to the land. In that time, the maritime losses around the point would amount to almost a million dollars (roughly $24.6 million in 2007, adjusted for inflation). Scheduled to begin in 1855, construction was delayed for a 17-year legal battle over the land on which the lighthouse was to sit.

In 1861, the *Sea Nymph* was the first of seven ships that went down off Point Reyes during the ensuing delay. The clipper ship ran aground after traveling enveloped in fog for ten days. The Captain, believing he was entering the Golden Gate, had the sails fully set when he struck Point Reyes beach with full force. Two years later, while on its way to San Francisco for a courtesy visit, the Russian warship *Novick* ran aground. The Captain was using a new English nautical chart labeled "corrections to 1865," showing a lighthouse already located on the Point Reyes headlands, seven years before its construction.

In November 1868, the Lighthouse Board began condemnation proceedings for the land. An advertisement ran in the Marin County newspaper for four months, as was required, to inform the public of the actions. This seemed to have lit a fire underneath the owners because they decided to sell. The sale gave the U.S. government 83 acres for the lighthouse reservation, access to Drakes Bay, and rights to firewood, water, and a granite quarry.

Originally, the plan was to build the lighthouse on the summit of Point Reyes, just like Point Bonita, but low-lying fog had often obscured the Bonita light. So learning from their mistakes, the Lighthouse Board chose a new site for the lighthouse at Point Reyes. Rather than install the light on the summit, it would be more effective relocated closer to the water. The site chosen to locate the tower was on a point that projected out about 275-feet below the summit. It was determined that the space needed to house a lighthouse the size of Cape Mendocino could be cleared on this rock solid section of the bluff.

Construction of the lighthouse proved to be arduous and dangerous; crews blasted, graded, and leveled a section of the cliff to accommodate the erection of the tower. A tramway built to carry the tools and materials down the cliff to the construction site helped ease the burden of workers.

In April 1870, San Francisco machinist, Joseph Bien contracted to oversee the construction of the new tower at Point Reyes. The structure would be identical to the tower at Cape Mendocino. Bien would also install the lighting apparatus. Bien began the fabrication of the forged iron plates at the San Francisco iron works, while waiting for the lens to arrive. These plates would make up the body of the squat tower and help protect against the severe weather on the point. The plates of the tower bed attached to bolts embedded into the stone and concrete foundation.

A combination wooden stairway and coal chute ran from the top of

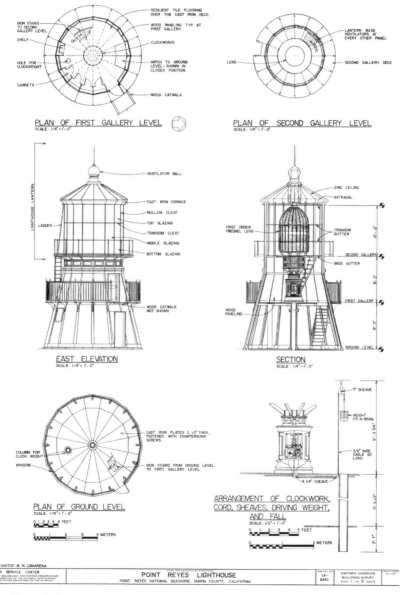

Point Reyes Diagram
Photo courtesy of The United States Lighthouse Society

the headland down to both sites. A small cable drawn flatcar, powered by a winch at the head of the stairs was used to transport items down the chute. Some sections of the chute dropped down at an incline of more than 50 degrees.

Light from the Point Reyes first order Fresnel lens first pierced the surrounding darkness on December 1, 1870. From the top of the bluff to the lighthouse was 300 steps, and to reach the fog signal located on the lower level required an additional 338 steps.

The station, painted white with red trim and red roofs, included the keeper's dwelling, which had 13 rooms, two coal houses, a blacksmith shop, a barn, and a distillate house. John C. Bull and his wife, Melissa, would become the first residents in the new home and John, the new light-keeper as of August 1870.

In 1871, preparation began on site for the installation of the Steam Fog-signal. A large cistern stored the water that was fed to the fog-signal through a galvanized iron pipe, which was securely fastened to the cliff. Duplicate fog signal equipment insured redundancy, so no time would be lost in the event of machine failure. Less than one year later, the fog-signal succumbed to fire, destroying the building and damaging the machinery. In September, a storage building containing 600 sacks of coal also burned and was a total loss. A new fog-signal once again broke the silence of the remote coast, on January 20, 1874.

In July 1874, the English ship *Warrior Queen* beached herself on the north side of Point Reyes, near Cleland's Ranch with no loss of life. The following day, second assistant Lincoln was presumed drowned, when he left the station to visit the shipwreck and never returned.

Behavior was always a problem in the early years of Point Reyes. Reports of drunkenness, abusiveness, and neglect overshadowed other events at the point. Third Assistant Parker, regularly neglected to show up for watches. He would also show up too drunk to work and was known to abandon his post. First assistant Rowe, prone to criticize everyone, would abuse others by calling them names and refusing to work. Both men lost their jobs, along with Wadsworth, the principal keeper.

In 1880, the Lighthouse Inspector, in the annual report to Congress, wrote;

> "Great complaint has been made, and now is made, of the inefficiency of the signal in this place, which at times cannot be heard a mile distant... Point Reyes is one of the most important points on the coast and the needs of navigation require

that its fog-signal should be in efficiency
second to none."

In January 1888, John C. Ryan became the new keeper at Point Reyes.
In the keepers' log Ryan stated, "I'm taking charge of this station I must
say that it is broken, filthy and almost a total wreck from end to end." One
of the sirens was inoperable, with pieces strewn about the station. Light-
keepers coaxed the north siren to work with a sledgehammer once every
half hour or so and as seldom as every hour and a half. The captain of the
cutter *Corwin* confirmed that his ship would sometimes lay off the point
for hours without hearing a sound.

The isolation of the station along with the heavy work and long hours
expected from the light-keepers, made finding competent men quite difficult
during its early days of operation. Captain Ludlow, from the Lighthouse
Board seemed to send out men who either could not or would not do the
required work. During an inspection, when told that the station was not
properly painted, Ryan assured inspector Ludlow that painting would be
attended to. Ryan also remarked that the sirens were in greater need of
attention, a remark for which Inspector Ludlow was not appreciative.

When a telegraph operator named Smails arrived, he informed Ryan
that Captain Ludlow hired him, and he was not taking orders from anyone
else. When the schooner *C. R. Bishop* was seen drifting toward the reef
one morning, Ryan went to Smails to have him telegraph San Francisco
for a tugboat to rescue the *Bishop*. Smails refused to get up and send the
telegraph. Eventually one of the local farmers drove to the nearest telegraph
station and sent for the tug, which arrived in time to save the *Bishop*. Two
other times Smails refused to send a telegraph or to allow Ryan's son, who
was also a telegraph operator, to send for needed assistance.

When Inspector Ludlow sent for Smails, Ryan appointed a replacement.
His course of action so angered the inspector that he sent him a letter
chastising him for daring to make the appointment. Ryan was handed his
dismissal soon after. That did not end the problems; there were refusals to
work by other light-keepers as well. In 1889, the constable in Olema took
an assistant light-keeper away when he "went crazy."

Duty at the Point Reyes station seemed to be a constant test of inner
strength. The men were continually isolated, performing routine tasks for
little pay. Much of the time the station was enveloped in fog that could last
for weeks at a time. Brutal winds blew past the point, beating their homes
and battering their senses. The intense monotony and loneliness could be
terribly oppressive.

The light-keepers at Point Reyes risked their lives every day, having to travel down hundreds of steps to get back and forth between the tower and their dwelling, sometimes during ferocious weather. Waves could splash 200-feet up the cliff and the wind could force a man to travel on his hands and knees to prevent from blowing off into the ocean. Protective railings, placed along some of the stairway, gave the men something to hold onto while attempting to traverse the stairs.

The great earthquake of 1906, with such destructive power, only bent the upper and lower guides of the Fresnel lens and displaced the lamp stand. The small iron tower designed to withstand the rigors of severe winds and storms came thorough unscathed. The quake also knocked the chimneys on the light-keeper's dwellings to the ground and cracked

Point Reyes Light Station
Photo courtesy of The United States Lighthouse Society

two cisterns. The keepers had the lens up and running again after only 11 minutes of lost time.

One would think that the installation of a lighthouse would minimize the number of shipwrecks in the surrounding area, but the peninsula proved to be the downfall of nearly 40 ships in the first 65 years of the station's operation.

Head light-keeper, P. Nilsson reported winds in excess of 100 mph in January 1916. The fences, chimneys, poles, and wires blew down, and the roof to the tank house was ripped off.

The Point Reyes Light Station was considered to be the most undesirable post in the district. The office had great difficulty in getting keepers to accept appointment to the station, and still greater difficulty in keeping them in the service after they had reported.

Sometime during the late 1920s, keeper Fred Kreth heroically rescued three men whose boat had crashed on the rocks below the light. The men from the life-saving station at Drakes Beach were unable to reach the frightened men, who clung to the rocks for over 20 hours. Kreth lowered a rope, climbed partway down the cliff, and guided the men up one by one.

Some of the tradition and esprit de corps associated with the Lighthouse Service was lost in the transition to the Coast Guard in 1939; the same year electricity came to the point. A small electric motor installed to rotate the lens apparatus replaced the need to use the original clockwork mechanism.

Military rotation now meant that younger men stationed at the lighthouse for a shorter period, would cause the eventual loss of the lighthouse "Old Timer."

As at other light stations, Point Reyes housed members of the Army during World War II, and when the war ended the soldiers left. The inevitability of automation hit Point Reyes in June of 1975. Thomas Smith, the last light-keeper of the station, turned off the first order Fresnel, marking an end to 105 years of service.

The establishment of Point Reyes National Seashore took place in 1962. The light station transferred from the U.S. Coast Guard to the National Park Service 15 years later. The Coast Guard is still responsible for maintaining the automated light and foghorn equipment, which is situated just below the station, fenced off from the public.

The rangers keep the first order Fresnel light and rotating mechanism operational and available as a backup should the primary navigational light fail. Restored in 2002, Point Reyes stands as a beautiful example of what a light-station on the California coast looked like during a previous life.

Point Arena

To some, the romantic image of a traditional lighthouse is exactly what is found at Point Arena, a tall cylindrical tower standing on the headland. At 115-feet, it shares the title of the tallest lighthouse structure in the State of California along with Pigeon Point, 180 miles south. The property is gated and inaccessible except during regular hours.

The Point is a narrow peninsula several hundred feet wide with a length of almost 800-feet. The vertical bluffs rise 50-feet from the surface of the water give drama to this tranquil spot. The great danger in approaching the point is Arena Rock. This massive rock is a mile long and sits six-feet under the surface of the water, a mile and a half off the headland.

In July 1869, workers, outfitted with all the necessary tools, together with a quantity of cement and lime, reached Point Arena. Derricks erected to hoist stones from the beach, delivered them to the cliffs above to be broken for concrete, and used to lay the foundations. More than 500 thousand bricks made on the grounds went into the construction of the tower. More than 100 thousand bricks used on the outside of the upper tower were shipped from San Francisco.

On May 1, 1870, a new light shone for the first time from its perch

Point Arena - August 1886
Photo courtesy of The United States Lighthouse Society

on Point Arena. A steam fog whistle went into operation the following November using cord wood to fuel the fire for the boilers. During years when more than one thousand hours of fog enveloped the region, the station would burn more than 100-tons of wood. To feed the thirsty boilers, two huge, underground cisterns ran from one edge of the point to the other, each lined with brick. The keepers' dwelling was a great two-and-a-half-story, brick residence that housed the entire four-man crew and all their wives and children.

Life could be terribly confining at an isolated light station, and Point Arena's single residence made privacy minimal. The big house, filled with adults and children, had thick walls, to cut down on sound, but the thin floors seemed to amplify sound. Noise would echo through the house, and an assistant light-keeper desperately trying to sleep after a long watch could have a difficult time.

The wind, as at many California lighthouses, could be particularly fierce. During the winter of 1879-80, all the fences blew down. In February 1880, one of the worst windstorms ever to hit the station took place, hurling everything movable in all directions. Sometimes there was no wind at all. During calm spells such as these, a heavy thick fog would creep in, enveloping the area. The light-keeper would then fire up the boilers in the fog signal building. Cold water would take 35 minutes to build up steam sufficient to blow the whistles. Sometimes, however, the water would still be warm from the previous day and could build ample steam pressure in as little as eight minutes.

The San Andreas Fault runs just off the point, giving the lighthouse an alarming vulnerability to earthquakes. A tremor not even felt in the fog signal building could have serious effects on the brick light tower.

A telephone was connected between the light-station and the town of Point Arena in November 1898. The phone was located in the keeper's quarters, and the other end of was placed in the office of the general telephone system, located in one of the Point Arena hotels.

The fog, wind, and sea all combined to make Point Arena a dangerous place for mariners. From the establishment of the station until 1900, there had been at least 13 major shipwrecks at or near the point. The light could make the sea-lanes safer, but it could never overcome all of the local hazards.

The great quake of 1906 left most of the town of Point Arena in ruins, and hit the brick lighthouse with tremendous force. When the quake ended, the lighthouse was still standing but it was shattered beyond repair. Initially tents pitched on the point served as shelter, but soon revealed their obvious inadequacies on such a windy point. The light-keepers had no choice but to move into the small, framed outbuildings that survived.

The Lighthouse Service funding came from Congress, in the form of appropriations passed annually. After the disaster, they were required to wait for six months until the next appropriation from Congress. Devastation, felt from Point Pinos to Cape Mendocino, affected wickies for the remainder of the year. The great quake had shaken the frugal Lighthouse Service as well, disrupting normal operations to such a great degree that it took an extreme departure from procedure. According to *Lighthouses and Lifeboats on the Redwood Coast* by Ralph C. Shanks; the Lighthouse Service, in an extraordinary move, informed the affected keepers to "proceed without further authority with what is absolutely necessary, reporting all liabilities incurred... make yourselves reasonably comfortable temporarily."

Following the quake, lumber schooners loaded with northern redwood to rebuild San Francisco increased the number of vessels passing the point. The lighthouse was still standing, but precariously, and it represented a serious challenge. The first thing was removing the lantern room from the tower. Problems had to be overcome considering that it was located 100-feet in the air, fixed on top of a tower riddled with cracks.

Many accounts were that the tower fell over during the earthquake, but this is not true. The earthquake had cracked the original tower in four places, each located at a landing and visible on both the inside and outside of the tower. The lighthouse-engineering department condemned the structure as being unsafe and slated the tower for destruction. It was necessary to raze the keeper's dwelling as well, displacing the four keepers and their families who resided there.

Although its relation to the epicenter of the quake was much farther than many of California's lighthouses, Point Arena would be one of the greatest California lighthouse casualties resulting from the quake. When bids went out for the work, the costs were considered too high by the Lighthouse Board. The decision was made to have the lighthouse-engineering department do the work themselves. Superintendent George Hooke was sent out from San Francisco and put in charge of demolishing the tower and keepers' quarters. When Walter White, the engineer at Lime Point Lighthouse, was asked to tear down the tower along with four other men, he took on the challenge. Because of the destruction, the men stayed at the Point Arena hotel for a few weeks and were transported by a team of horses to the light station. Six carpenters, brought in from San Francisco complimented the remainder of the crew made up of Point Arena locals.

The first job was to create temporary housing for the keepers and construction workers. An 80-foot building constructed for the keepers sat not too far from a 60-foot bunkhouse built for the crew of 30. After the men had all moved into the new housing structures, the job of tearing down the tower and light-keeper's dwelling proceeded.

The lantern and lens were the first removed, each piece carefully marked and lowered from the tower. The lantern was then installed on a 30-foot temporary tower, housing a second order lens. Exhibited beginning January 5, 1907, the temporary tower was used until the completion of the work. The ruined first order lens was packed and shipped to the general lighthouse depot.

Piece by piece items were lowered from the tower using a 25-foot mast. The iron window frames, landings and iron staircase were all preserved for use in the new tower. Now jacks, drills, and sledgehammers were used to loosen the nearly one million bricks that were dropped to the ground below, until the whole tower had been dismantled. All of the brick masonry taken from the old tower and light-keepers' dwelling, that was suitable for future use, was cleaned and stored. All the remaining debris that could not be salvaged was pushed over the cliff and into the sea.

Operations were suspended for several months due to lack of funds. When the work continued, the original center post became the center of

Point Arena - temporary tower, March 1907
Photo courtesy of The United States Lighthouse Society

the new foundation. The brick structure had proven itself too rigid and brittle to withstand the awesome force of the quake. Engineers now faced a problem of how to build a new lighthouse that could withstand a major earthquake. Traditional masonry and stone construction techniques were discarded for a radical new idea to construct a 115-foot high light tower using reinforced concrete. Scaffolding soon surrounded the sentinel, rising more than 100-feet in the air. The threading of the metal rebar and the pouring of cement was all handwork. An elevator pulled by a mule, raised the wheelbarrows of cement up to the landings to be poured into forms.

When the scaffolding began to come down in November of 1907, it revealed the first reinforced concrete lighthouse in the United States. Hundreds of bags of cement went into the construction of the tower, sidewalks, and foundations for the four dwellings.

The staircase and landings were reconstructed inside the tower, which was topped with the original lantern. The first order lens was then installed, placed floating in a bath of mercury. Mercury provided a virtually frictionless method of rotation; balanced so precisely that any disruption would tip the lens like a boat on water.

In 1908, four private dwellings took the place of the original keepers' dwelling. The front of each of the stately two-story houses was adorned with a long wooden sun porch that ran the full length of the house. On January 15, 1908, keeper Robert H. Williams and his three assistants began operation of the new lighthouse at Point Arena.

After construction was complete and the men were discharged, Walter White stayed on. White would spend a total of two years at Point Arena, painting the station inside and out, including the tower, dwellings, roofs, stairs, landings, and fog engines. Walter White would then move to Point Cabrillo to construct the new lighthouse at Mendocino.

Bill Owens transferred to Point Arena Light Station as second assistant light-keeper in July 1937. According to his wife Isabel in her unpublished memoirs,

> "We came to California in 1926. He worked at the Bethlehem Shipyard in San Francisco for about four years. He liked to fish, and on Sundays, he would go to Angel Island and spend the day fishing. He became acquainted with the lighthouse keeper stationed there and decided that was the life for him. He could spend his spare time fishing and there would be the security of a government job."

His first duty was at Point Conception Light Station as third assistant keeper, then onto Point Sur and then Point Arena.

Isabel went on to say,

> "Mr. Elmer Williams, the head keeper, came out to meet us. Bill gave him his transfer order. The yards, front and back, were large and fenced in with a picket fence in front and a high board fence in the back with two high lattice fences, one on each side of the house, separating the front yard from the back yard. There was plenty of room, even for our family of seven. There was a very large kitchen, large dining room, average sized living room, utility room, pantry, bathroom, two bedrooms, a sun porch and two open porches (one in front and one in back), all downstairs. Upstairs there were two more bedrooms."

The Coast Guard assumed control of the light in 1939, creating a very different atmosphere from the old Lighthouse Service. All new keepers would be members of the Coast Guard. The existing civilian keepers were allowed to remain and given the choice of enlisting or remaining a civilian. One of the first duties under Coast Guard control was having the polished brass work of the lens painted a military grey. Many of the great keepers were distressed and bitter at the changes taking place. The Coast Guard had absorbed the Lighthouse Service but the same civilian personnel operated the light stations. The light-keepers were now under the command of Coast Guard officers, who lacked knowledge of lighthouses that the old timers possessed. Some Coast Guard officers appreciated the expertise of the seasoned keepers, gaining the respect of those who could pass on their knowledge and expertise. One advantage in the change was that the Coast Guard was much more generous with supplies than the frugal Lighthouse Service had ever been.

For the long-term, the merger had caused a decrease in fully trained personnel. USCG enlisted men served a short tour of duty. A lack of time to train these men as competent assistant keepers caused the skill levels at some light stations to decline significantly. The Coast Guard came to depend upon the highly skilled specialists from San Francisco or Humboldt Bay when it came to the more difficult maintenance and repair work. Fortunately, Point Arena was under the command of Bill Owens and continued to function as a highly efficient station.

At the beginning of World War II the light stations along the Pacific coast were especially alert, since California is the closest point to Japan on the United States mainland.

Early one morning at daybreak, Bill Owens was on watch, Isabel was working in the kitchen looking out to sea when they both saw something rise from the ocean west of the fog signal building. They believed it to be a Japanese submarine, but since it was about three miles from shore, they could not be sure. All too aware of his civic duty, Owens rushed into the house to phone Navy headquarters in San Francisco. The Officer of the Day refused to believe the keeper and told him, "There are no Japanese submarines in these waters...go back to bed and get some more sleep." A day or two after the incident, the American lumber schooner *Emidio* came under torpedo attack by a Japanese submarine off Cape Mendocino, north of Point Arena. Newspaper accounts published two days later included pictures of Japanese submarines, one of which was identical to the vessel the Owens's had seen. The next day some officers came to the station to swear Owens to secrecy. When Owens asked how long they wanted him to keep quiet about it, instructions were – "until after the war."

Not too long after that, Owens received orders from the office to keep the cars filled with gas at all times, and ready to go in case of an evacuation. During the war the light never went dark, though the radio beacon had its range reduced to ten-miles, so that only coasting vessels could use it. With anticipation of a possible enemy attack, mandatory blackouts were routine, throwing the entire coast into darkness with the exception of the great light. A record number of people came to live at the point during the war. Japanese military operations were taking place just miles off shore, so the Coast Guard established a beach patrol all along the California coast.

Enlisted men moved into two of the dwellings at Point Arena. Young Coast Guardsmen operated a lookout station at the light near the fog signal and patrolled beaches and headlands north and south of the light. Hundreds of miles of even the most isolated coastline were under surveillance, and the beach patrol at Point Arena was but one small link in the vast network covering the state. Isabel Owens remembered,

> "There were three systems of watches. The lighthouse crew had to report by phone to San Francisco everything sighted on the ocean or in the air. There was a civilian watch about one mile from the

lighthouse. A group of about 30 soldiers sent to the station temporarily while barracks were set up for them elsewhere. They stayed in a couple of houses that were empty. When their arrangements were completed, they rode horses to keep watch along the coast. At all times they had one man riding south and another riding north. A few miles south of Point Arena was the Olson Sheep Ranch. Mr. Olson was riding his horse around the ranch to check on the sheep. As he got close to the bluff, he heard a humming noise. He rode closer to see what it was. He saw a Japanese sub sitting in close to the bluff, apparently recharging their batteries. He called the District Office to report it. They sent a plane up to bomb it, the first one missed, but the second went down the hatch, putting an end to the submarine. One or two days after the sinking the newspaper printed pictures of two types of Japanese subs. One of them was exactly like what I'd seen."

The most dramatic shipwreck to take place at or near Point Arena was the stranding of the British Freighter *Pacific Enterprise* during a blinding fog. The light was on in the tower, and the fog signal was bellowing its call out over the ocean. The *Pacific Enterprise* found itself stranded in the outlying rocks of Point Arena, within plain view of the lighthouse. The ship's Captain, M. E. Cogle, a veteran of 40 years, was on his final voyage, and he believed from the fog signal he heard that he was just off the Farallon Islands, 20 miles away. Reaching shore safely were 54 crew members and five passengers but her cargo of lumber, canned salmon, grain, and metals would be lost. Joan Owens, one of Bill and Isabel's six daughters was in the backyard and heard the ship's horn blowing. "It sounded like it was coming from the other side of the fence, but it was so foggy, I couldn't see a thing."

Bill and Isabel Owens were having breakfast and heard the freighter as it approached. Isabel thought it was "like the ship was right in our backyard." Owens ran to the fog signal building to alert the lifeboat station, but before he arrived, he heard the sound of the ship striking Arena Rock.

Point Arena - October 1907 - Note the temporary tower to the left
Photo courtesy of The United States Lighthouse Society

Owens notified the station as well as Coast Guard headquarters in San Francisco, whose response was swift. A 36-foot motor lifeboat dispatched to the scene from the lifeboat station, and big cutters were sent from San Francisco Bay. The motor lifeboat was on the scene in minutes, finding the 454-foot long British freighter *Pacific Enterprise* stranded on the offshore rocks. When the fog lifted, the stranded ship lay just beyond the lighthouse and for a moment in time, the *Pacific Enterprise* became the story to cover.

Suddenly the Owens family was having their 15 minutes of fame, with reporters, photographers, film crews, and curiosity seekers. Bill Owens found himself with an expanded role as hundreds of people showed up with no sense of propriety. Even keeping the gate closed to the lighthouse station was useless because people just parked their cars outside the fence and came on in. In a little over a week, the ocean had beaten the ship to pieces. The light-keepers saw the ship break in half, and the aft section sink; a few days later the bow was gone.

It was exciting for the family when the film showed at the little theater in Point Arena. Seeing Bill Owens interviewed by the reporters made everyone feel like celebrities. Owens received the Albert Gallatin Award in 1963, for his long, loyal, and faithful service to our nation and devotion to duty.

Automation came to Point Arena in 1977. The Fresnel was retired and replaced with a small beacon. In 1984, due to their historic preservation and educational efforts, an organization called the Point Arena Lighthouse Keepers acquired the light station as part of a 25-year land lease from the Coast Guard and the Department of Transportation. In September 2004, the mercury float used to rotate the first order Fresnel lens for 98 years became the last mercury float in the United States removed from service.

Point Arena Light Station
Photo courtesy of The United States Lighthouse Society

POINT CABRILLO

Less than four miles from the village of Mendocino the Point Cabrillo Nature Preserve can be found, 300 acres of coastal property including 30.5 acres of the Point Cabrillo Light Station. The waters immediately along the Preserve are also a Marine Reserve established in the 1970s by the State Department of Fish and Game. The Preserve is home to deer, other mammals, reptiles, and an incredibly diverse bird population that includes Red Shouldered Hawk, Coopers Hawk, Kestrel, Northern Harrier, Osprey, White-tailed Kite, Pelagic Cormorants, and Songbirds.

From the parking lot, the lighthouse is a half-mile walk. Two routes are available; the paved access road is the most direct, or you can take the walking trail through the Preserve. The trail winds along the bluffs overlooking the ocean and is home to many birds and animals.

Point Cabrillo is one of the most complete light stations in the state, and a restoration effort has brought this magnificent historic complex slowly back to the way it appeared in 1935. The restoration began with the blacksmith shop and the oil house (currently housing the Coast Guard Loran and VHF Marine Radio) completed in 1998. Work in the lighthouse itself began with the lens. In August of 1998, a third order Fresnel, one of only three lenses in America made by the English firm of *Chance Brothers,* was removed and cleaned piece by piece. The lens, reinstalled as the primary aid to navigation just in time for the 90th anniversary of Point Cabrillo, now rests in its home of almost 100 years. The lighthouse doubles as a gift-shop and museum offering a live video feed from the cupola to view the lens as it rotates.

As a Federal Aid to Navigation, requirements dictate that the light in the Fresnel lens derive its power from electricity. Since the lamp conversion from kerosene to electricity took place in 1935, that year became the perfect snapshot in time to represent the station. At that time the station still appeared as it did in 1909. During this brief period, the station had all of its original buildings displaying their original colors. Maintaining attention to detail and meticulous standards have assured that the restoration retains as much of the original structures as possible.

The San Andreas Fault runs north and south about four miles off the coast. Over millennia, as the tectonic plates slid past each other, they created a series of marine terraces. Over time, this shift pushed up silt and soft soils to produce the bluffs where the light station resides. These dramatic cliffs surrounding the lighthouse and preserve are constantly eroding. The continual pounding of surf against the cliffs, undermines the stability of the earth. Even though work has been done to introduce native plants along some of the cliff areas to help support the surrounding soil, Mother Nature will eventually win out.

Point Cabrillo provides peaceful serenity. With nothing that resembles a bustling civilization nearby, one can relax, reflect, and enjoy the sounds of birds, wind, and surf.

The great San Francisco earthquake had created a tremendous demand for lumber and building supplies along the coast, increasing traffic to an all time high. In June 1906, Congress approved the construction of a light station at Point Cabrillo.

The property, purchased in January 1908, allowed construction to begin in August. A small incline railway used to haul gravel up from the beach was constructed on the cliff north of the lighthouse. The first keeper of the Point Cabrillo Lighthouse, Wilhelm Baumgartner, lit the third order Fresnel for the first time on June 10, 1909.

Various problems were apparent the first year; the windows in the dwellings leaked when the rains arrived, the fireplaces did not draw, and the road was in need of completion, as was an operational oil house.

Located between Fort Bragg and Mendocino, the lighthouse consists of a 47-foot-tall octagonal tower attached to the fog signal building.

Illuminated by a kerosene oil lamp, the third order Fresnel lens was housed in a lantern room surrounded by a balcony.

Point Cabrillo Lighthouse
Photo courtesy of The United States Lighthouse Society

The lens was mounted on top of four tiers of brass pillars, and rotated on a set of ball bearings. A 65-80 pound weight, attached to the end of a chain, ran down through every floor of the light tower, driving the clockwork mechanism. The clockworks needed to be wound every two hours to restore the weight to the top of the tower. A deep hole, cut out of the concrete foundation in later years, allowed the addition of chain length to create more time between windings.

Only three British-made Fresnel lenses ever went into use in the United States. The other two are, a first order lens installed in the Heceta Head Lighthouse in Oregon and a second order range light used at the Battery Point Lighthouse on Staten Island, New York.

To the east of the lighthouse is where the keeper's dwellings are located, all in a row. The head keepers' dwelling, erected in the center with its enclosed front porch, is perhaps a touch fancier than the other two homes. The dwellings for the assistants were two-story homes with porches, brick fireplaces, and large fenced-in yards, each with their own storage shed. Behind the sheds, lay a cistern, water tank and pump house.

Point Cabrillo was a desirable post for light-keepers, with generally good weather, easy access, good soil, and plenty of water. The proximity to schools, stores, and churches made life considerably less difficult than at other stations.

Light-keepers could have three cows, pigs, and all the chickens they desired. Soon, keeper Miller had provided a home for 400 chickens in his backyard. The barn was used as the slaughterhouse and chicken coop, and the basements of the dwellings were where ham and venison cured. Vegetables, tended in the backyards of the dwellings, provided the families with fresh produce. Trellises abundant with beautiful flowers filled the backyard gardens with brilliant color in the spring.

Erosion was just as much a concern in 1909, as it is now. The ground surrounding the cliffs could become quite soft during the rainy season. From time to time, a cow or horse standing as far as 15-feet from the edge would plummet into the sea below when the earth gave way.

Light-keepers found their lives changed with the new electric light and motor drive mechanism installed in 1935. It was no longer necessary to give the lens the same attention. No adjustment to the ventilation was required to keep the oil lamp burning correctly. No longer did they wind the clockwork motor drive every two hours, although the light-keepers maintained the clockwork in good repair as a backup. They also kept a Coleman lantern in the tower storage cabinet filled with fuel. The fog-signal equipment also changed dramatically. No longer was time required for the gas engine to fill the compressor with enough air to blow the sirens.

The new electric motor and diaphone produced the fog signal at the flip of a switch. The original equipment was maintained in good operating condition, just in case.

The residents of Point Cabrillo were a bit on edge the first few months of World War II, fearing spies from Japan landing on our shores. When standing their watch alone, keepers came armed with a hunting rifle. Lookout towers and barracks were established at regular intervals along the coast, and often took advantage of existing life saving stations or light stations. Point Cabrillo, selected as an outpost, had U.S. Coast Guard Quonset huts installed at the station, housing over a dozen men who patrolled the beaches and headlands. The blacksmith shop served as a kitchen and during the holidays, the keeper's families welcomed the men into their homes.

Just one fifth of a mile off Point Cabrillo the seabed falls off to a depth of 180-feet. Waves coming in from the sea can hit that underwater wall with such power that the water, having nowhere else to go, is capable of flooding over the bluffs more than 50-feet above sea level and threatening the lighthouse. Just such an occurrence took place in February 1960, when a huge storm struck the Mendocino coast late in the afternoon. By evening breakers were striking against the point with tremendous force, ripping out large sections of earth and hurling them into the sea. So high were the waves, they washed across the grasslands actually crashing against the lighthouse. The light, turned on early in the storm, remained on during the gale, but keeper Owens notified the Coast Guard that he could not start the fog signal because the waves were washing against the lighthouse. The doors of the fog signal building along with sections of the wooden siding peeled away under the force of the wind and water. Even the big diesel generators and air compressors slid across the mud-covered floor of the fog signal building. The bolts that mounted the equipment to the cement were sheared off completely. Almost a foot of rocks, gravel, and sand were on the floor of the lighthouse, and debris was scattered all across the station. Huge rocks carried onto the land by the waves were deposited on the bluff, including a huge boulder that was at least 50-feet from the edge of the cliff.

Bill Owens retired as the last civilian light-keeper in California in 1963, after 32 years of service. Bill Owens had started his career at Point Conception Lighthouse and was later stationed at Point Sur, Point Arena, and finally Point Cabrillo. Owens raised his six daughters, Shirley, Sarah, Dixie, Diana, and the twins, Joan and Jean with his devoted wife Cora Isabel.

The familiar sound of the foghorns disappeared in 1963, replaced with a sounding apparatus on an offshore buoy. Automation of the light came in 1973, the Fresnel lens, protected by a surrounding curtain, was replaced with an aero-marine-type rotating beacon mounted on the roof.

Between 1988 and 1991 the California State Coastal Conservancy acquired 270 acres of land around the light station and finally in 1992 negotiated a transfer of the Light Station property and buildings from the Coast Guard to the Conservancy. The Conservancy then created the Non Profit, the North Coast Interpretive Association to manage the new preserve and the historic light station ensuring public access and development of a long term restoration program for the light station.

In 1989, in a move that raised the ire of locals, the Coast Guard announced plans to move the original Fresnel lens (unused since automation came in 1972) to a museum in Virginia. Local opposition won out and prevented the removal of the lens. Over the winter of 1998/99 the lens and lantern room were carefully restored. The 90 year old lens was then reactivated by the Coast Guard as the federal aid to navigation at Point Cabrillo. The lantern room and beautiful third order Fresnel lens are today maintained by members of the local Coast Guard Auxiliary Flotilla. Point Cabrillo transferred from the Coastal Conservancy to California State Parks in 2002, and the Point Cabrillo Light-keeper's Association came into being.

In 2004 the east keeper's dwelling was restored and opened as a museum showing how the keepers' families lived in the 1930's. In 2006, Point Cabrillo opened the newly restored head light-keeper's house as a bed and breakfast, complete with early 1900's furnishings and antiques. All donations and proceeds brought in are invested in the restoration, reconstruction, maintenance, educational programs, and operational management of the light station.

Punta Gorda

Punta Gorda is maintained by the U.S. Bureau of Land Management. This historic site, located in Kings Range, California's Lost Coast, sits 12 miles south of Cape Mendocino. It is the second most remote lighthouse location on the California mainland, Point Conception being more remote but completely inaccessible to the public.

This is not a day trip. One must be prepared, in relatively good physical shape and feel comfortable driving for hours on steep, windy mountain roads. After leaving Highway 101, there are no amenities to be found. There are also short stretches of road that have no pavement, many of which are on steep 180 degree turns.

The destination is Mattole State Beach, a small clearing just over the dunes from the ocean. Basic rest rooms with no electrical or running water are available, but this is not the final destination. The hike is a three and a half mile trek down the beach, mostly along the sheer cliffs that buffer the ocean. High tide regularly makes the hike impassible so checking the tide schedule is necessary. There is usually a tide report on the big information sign. If you leave at the wrong time you can find yourself stranded.

The remains of Punta Gorda Lighthouse, recently restored and painted, are empty, just a cement shell, no doors, windows, or lens. Visitors can climb the stairs to the cupola, and gaze out to sea. A short distance down the hill, is the oil house that still holds the tremendous oil drums that once stored kerosene used to fuel the light, although time and rust are taking

Punta Gorda Light Station
Photo courtesy of The United States Lighthouse Society

their toll. This is one of the few stations where the tanks are intact, not many oil drums remain, you can find many oil houses, but the drums are long since gone. The point is peaceful, as not many people visit this remote lighthouse location.

In 1907, 87 souls were lost from the passenger ship *Columbia*. This was the latest in a string of ill-fated ships that went down on the jagged reefs off the point. The Lighthouse Board finally approved the building of a lighthouse at Punta Gorda near the rocky Kings Range.

Plagued with dangerous reefs and fierce wind, Punta Gorda also lies beyond a creek, which during the winter makes this remote location almost impassable. Construction materials, brought in via a high wire suspended between the beach, and a schooner half a mile away, were then dragged down the beach on a horse-drawn sled to the site.

First lit on January 15, 1912, Punta Gorda housed a fourth order Fresnel. For sustenance, these frontiersmen tended cattle, goats, and chickens. During periods of good weather, they could make the 11 mile journey to the small town of Petrolia for supplies.

The stretch of desolate beach below the lighthouse was home to three residences, a blacksmith shop, a barn, three sheds, and the fog signal building. Electricity never made it to this remote location. Known by light-keepers as the "loneliest lighthouse," Punta Gorda also received the nickname "the Alcatraz of Lighthouses" as well.

The deactivation of the lighthouse happened in 1951, when an ocean buoy replaced it as the aid to navigation. During the late 1960s, hippies moved into the dwellings. In 1970, after occupying the residence for several years, local authorities evicted the squatters and burned down the buildings.

LIGHTSHIP WLV 605

The lightship WLV 605 is located in Oakland's Jack London Square, hidden behind the *Potomac,* Franklin Delano Roosevelt's private Presidential Yacht. The lightship is located on the very western edge of Jack London Square and kept in meticulously restored shape. Tours of the lightship are available from excellent docents like John Byrne, who spent time stationed on lightships and gives an insight to life at sea that makes the tour well worthwhile.

The story of California's lighthouses would be incomplete without mentioning the lightships that once protected our shore. That would be a disservice to the brave men stationed at these outposts and neglects an important part of how the Lighthouse Service/Coast Guard helped guide the ships at sea. Lightships served the same function as lighthouses. They were equipped with lights, fog signals, and radio beacons, sitting anchored at points where it was impracticable to build a lighthouse. Lightships marked the entrance to important harbors and estuaries, or protected ships against hazardous shoals or reefs. All United States lightships were painted red, with the name of the ship painted in white, six and a half feet tall, on each side.

Lightships were sometimes reassigned. Old ships retired and new ships built, so several ships could have occupied one lightship location. Two lightships stationed off the coast of California protected the incoming ships, one outside San Francisco Bay, which began operation in April 1898, and one off Blunt's Reef, which was anchored in 1905. The primary concern of those stationed aboard a lightship was to keep her "on station." If the ship ever moved from its precise location, all other services took a back seat until they could regain the charted position.

Men stationed on a lightship dealt with more dangers than its land based counterpart; lightships stayed on station no matter what the conditions. Fierce storms have caused more than one lightship to capsize and sink. The main anchor and chain were massive, shaped like a mushroom and weighed 6,000 to 8,000 pounds. The anchor, connected to a chain six to ten times longer than the depth of the water, had links weighing about 14-pounds each. Additional chain, let out during winter storms, relieved the strain put upon the ship by the pitching and rolling of the sea. The length was decreased during the fair summer weather.

Blunt's reef is made up of two rocks covered at high tide. They sit about 200-yards from each other and are approximately three miles from the Cape Mendocino lighthouse. The Blunt's Reef lightship, anchored two miles from the outer rock, warned ships of this hazardous reef. A number of sunken rocks and ledges make the area between the reef and Cape Mendocino extremely dangerous especially when enveloped in fog.

In 1916, the liner *Bear* struck Blunt's Reef in a heavy fog. The crew launched 12 lifeboats, two headed for shore but never made it, two women and three men drowned after the crafts were swamped on the rocks. The remaining ten life boats found their way to the Blunt's Reef Lightship, and the crew was able to get all 150 survivors on board. The passengers were later transferred to the tugboat *Relief* and the steamer *Grace Dollar*.

When a lightship needed to return to port, a relief ship would anchor in its place. During the trip to port, the lightship would fly a series of flags to identify them as not in service.

On December 20, 1941, just 13 days after the attack on Pearl Harbor, the Japanese submarine *I-17* shelled and sunk the unarmed U.S. tanker *Emidio* off Cape Mendocino. The crew from the Blunt's Reef Lightship rescued 31 survivors.

The 128-foot Lightship designated as WAL 605 was constructed in 1950, and had an electric lens lantern on the foremast only. Twin diaphones were mounted aft of the pilothouse. Firing up the high recovery air compressor to amass the thousands of cubic feet of air needed to sound the diaphone, created dread among the crew members. Everyone knew when they heard the engines start; they had 15 minutes before the torture of the horns would begin. The blast, clearly heard five miles away, had a sound

Lightship WLV 605
Photograph by Kent Weymouth

level of 140 decibels, almost 20 decibels louder than a 707. Onboard there was nowhere to escape; the entire ship would tremble. Dishes in the galley would rattle, items would vibrate off tables, and the decks and bulkheads would modulate. The signal sounded every 30 seconds, and in a heavy fog, the torturous signal could blast for days.

In 1960, the WAL 605 had its assignment changed to Blunts Reef, where it replaced the LV 523, which was becoming a Relief Ship. The designation of WAL 605 changed to WLV 605 in 1965. After nine years anchored at Blunts Reef, the Lightship WLV 605 became a Relief Ship. The job was now to relieve all west coast lightships when they left station for overhaul.

The ship, decommissioned by the Coast Guard in 1976, moved to Olympia, Washington, the following year. After an unsuccessful attempt at turning the ship into a floating museum, the ship sold to Mr. Alan Hosking of Woodside. In December 1986, Mr. Hosking donated the ship to the United States Lighthouse Society. The Lightship WLV 605 was designated a national historical landmark in December 1989. The San Francisco Bar Station Lightship retired in May 1971.

Lightship WLV 605 sleeping quarters
Photograph by Kent Weymouth

CAPE MENDOCINO

Cape Mendocino Lighthouse
Photo courtesy of The United States Lighthouse Society

In 1948, the first order lens from the Cape Mendocino lighthouse moved to the entrance of the Humboldt County Fairgrounds in Ferndale, where it sits on display in a beautiful replica of the original tower. This little building is located at the entrance to the fairgrounds and acts as a ticket booth during the fair. The town of Ferndale is one of the true gems of California. This charming community has maintained the architecture of early America's Victorian era. Modern stores and restaurants are curiously absent in this quaint little town, but straw hats can be found in the general store on Main Street.

The original location of the Cape Mendocino lighthouse is south of town. The area bears almost no trace of once having housed this squat iron tower. The compound that stood on this hill has been wiped away. The site, closed to the public, shows scars where roads led to buildings that once stood, but nature overtakes the scene and with each passing season the site is less noticeable.

This little lighthouse tower now sits on Point Delgado in Mal Combs Park in Shelter Cove, south from the original location in a small open field with walkways and picnic tables.

Although first authorized following the coastal survey of 1850-51, delays created by the Civil War put off the building of the lighthouse. In the decade proceeding construction, 30 ships went down in the area. It had become obvious that building a lighthouse at Cape Mendocino to protect the maritime commerce was essential.

Construction on the Cape Mendocino Lighthouse finally began in 1867. In September, while bringing construction materials, the supply ship *Shubrick* struck a rock 13 miles south of Punta Gorda. The captain managed to steer the vessel onto the beach and soft sand. Salvaging the tender was successful, but the cargo was lost.

Located on the western most point of California, Cape Mendocino can have fierce weather conditions and dangerous seas. To the north, brutal winds and heavy rains are common, to the south; dense fog is more prevalent, creating very unpredictable weather on the cape. Off the coast of Cape Mendocino sits Sugar Loaf Island, rising 326-feet from the water's surface. To the south are; Beach Rock, Fauntleroy Rock, and the Great Breaks. Three miles northwest of Cape Mendocino sits Blunts Reef once home to the Lightship WLV 605.

Work on the lighthouse was difficult due to the remote location and elevation of the site. Cape Mendocino is one continuous slope, so it was necessary to use mules and even a derrick to get materials up the mountain to the site. During the summer the earth was a hard pack, but when winter hit, the earth would give way to mud slides and slip outs. The location planned for the lighthouse was too soft and unstable even for a small tower. Crews removed the soil down to bedrock and refilled the hole with cement. The cement pad was extended out to provide a walkway around the tower. Cut into the hillside behind the tower, a stone and mortar retaining wall was erected, to prevent slide outs.

Cape Mendocino and Point Reyes are the only two California lighthouses built of forged iron. This technique, employed to help resist the brutal weather found at the cape, consisted of 16 plates of forged iron. The first and second levels of the little tower were prefabricated at the San Francisco Iron Works. They were then shipped from San Francisco and hauled up the steep cliffs to Cape Mendocino. The iron tower, then bolted to the massive cement pad for extra strength, could hold up against the brutal winds found at the cape. A fog signal at Cape Mendocino was impractical due to the distant proximity of the shipping lanes. It was impossible to hear so far offshore, so a whistling buoy anchored beyond the reef did the job. On December 1, 1867, the Cape Mendocino light, a 43-foot tall 16-sided cast iron tower, began its operation.

Almost immediately, cracks began to appear in the new residence.

During the winter, as the ground started to settle, problems began. The Cape Mendocino compound sat on 171-acres of steep, sandy, gravelly fields in an area of California that is quite susceptible to earthquakes due to the juxtaposition of three major geological plates. In 1870, an earthquake destroyed the original quarters. Rebuilt in 1872, the following year a moderate earthquake cracked the ground, opening up a crevasse in the earth just 15-feet from the tower. The crack was filled with cement, returning stability to the ground. Wind and rain proved to be the greatest concern at the cape. Rain saturating the ground, created settling in the buildings, which began to shift and crack breaking windows, and collapsing the chimneys. The replacement dwelling was no match for the winds and soon began to shake apart. Light-keepers and their families often huddled in the tiny lighthouse to avoid the violent wind and rains. In the tower they knew they would be safe.

Wind was the greatest fear of the residents of Cape Mendocino. So ferocious was the wind that getting from the dwellings to the lighthouse during a storm could be a life-threatening act. A small watch house was built adjacent to the tower and equipped with a bed that could accommodate keepers during brutal storms with long periods of heavy wind or rain. The 1883 Lighthouse Board Annual Report to Congress said, "This is probably the windiest site occupied by any light station in the country."

Arriving on the tender *Manzanita* in 1881, Lighthouse Inspector D. J. McDougal drowned, along with three other men, when their small launch capsized off Cape Mendocino. As legend has it, gold carried in his money belt, to pay the keepers, dragged him down to his eventual demise. After the accident, McDougal's wife Kate became the appointed keeper of Mare Island Light where she remained for 35 years.

Conditions on the cape were merciless for the light-keepers and their families. Windstorms of great intensity broke windows, while earthquakes rattled and cracked the ceilings and warped the floors. Significant damage to all of the structures facilitated the rebuilding of the dwellings three separate times within a 40 year period.

During the late 1890s, the assistant light-keeper and his family had to resort to living in the oil house. The Lighthouse Board had deemed the oil house to be "almost uninhabitable on account of its bad and unsanitary conditions." For ten years, the light-keepers petitioned the Lighthouse Board for the funds to build a new dwelling for the assistant light-keeper and his family, but to no avail. Year after year the annual reports pleaded for a new dwelling, but the family remained in the oil house. It is no wonder that the inspections also consistently reported the health of lighthouse staff as "poor" or "fair" during this period. The 1906 earthquake demolished the oil house and badly damaged the head keeper's dwelling. Finally the building of new quarters for the light-keepers and their families was approved. In 1939, the addition of a dirt road allowed the light-keepers the ability to drive right up to the station.

A small beacon replaced the huge first order Fresnel lens in 1948. When electricity and automation made its way to the cape in 1951 the station was deactivated. In 1962, the Coast Guard burned the quarters and filled in the basements in order to prevent squatters. The light remained in operation until 1971, when the Coast Guard replaced it with a pair of automated beacons mounted atop a pole 515-feet above sea level.

The original structure remained on the hillside but was ravaged by the salt air, rain, mud slides, and earthquakes. Concerned about the loss of the Lighthouse, the Coast Guard went searching for interested parties in the early 1990s to restore and maintain the aging structure. A group of concerned citizens in Humboldt County formed an organization called the "Cape Mendocino Lighthouse Preservation Society - Shelter Cove" to vie for the opportunity to save the historical structure. After a lengthy process, the society became the choice to restore and maintain the lighthouse. In 1998, The California National Guard supplied a helicopter to relocate the lantern room from its original home to Shelter Cove.

Volunteers disassembled the lower portion of the structure and hauled the plates to Whitethorn Construction Company. For almost two years, volunteers scraped and cleaned the iron lighthouse, piece by piece. Reassembly, completed in May of 2000, allowed the lighthouse to open for visitors. The little tower, staffed by volunteers daily from Memorial Day to Labor Day, is also open on weekends during the off-season.

TABLE BLUFF LIGHTHOUSE

Table Bluff Lighthouse
Photo courtesy of The United States Lighthouse Society

In the beautiful historic town of Eureka, located in the parking lot of the marina on Woodley Island, stands all that is left of the Table Bluff lighthouse. Peering out over Humboldt Bay, is a statue of a fisherman in his boat, casting out his net, a tribute to those local fishermen lost at sea. A more picturesque view of the lighthouse tower can be found from downtown Eureka, looking across the water.

In 1885, after 29 years of service, the original lighthouse guarding the North Spit of Humboldt Bay succumbed to natural forces. Chosen by the Lighthouse Board to protect the entrance to Humboldt Bay, North Spit had proved a poor choice. The lighthouse had been roundly criticized for having been located at too low an elevation. After the 1877 earthquake and subsequent flooding in 1885, the Lighthouse Board made the decision to move the lighthouse. The location chosen to relocate the light was Table Bluff, a cliff located on the south end of Humboldt Bay. Just to the north of Table Bluff is the quarry where men cut the enormous stones to be used for the St. George Reef Lighthouse.

This new sea coast light was patterned after the Ballast Point Lighthouse in San Diego. The station consisted of; the keepers' quarters built around the 35-foot light tower, quarters for the assistants, the fog-signal building, two wash houses, an oil house, and a carpenter shop. The new lighthouse at Table Bluff first shone its fourth order Fresnel lens on October 31, 1892.

Soon after the light had made its move, it became apparent that North Spit still required a fog signal. A new fog signal without a light was built in 1904, near the location of the original lighthouse and officially took the place of the old station.

On the afternoon of December 20, 1941, the *Emidio*, a tanker for General Petroleum, became the victim of a torpedo attack by a Japanese submarine off Blunts Reef near Cape Mendocino. In *Lighthouses and Lifeboats on the Redwood Coast* by Ralph C. Shanks, he states that the Table Bluff radio station received the following message: "STEAMSHIP EMIDIO OFF BLUNTS REEF LIGHTSHIP NEED ASSISTANCE AT ONCE... EMIDIO LAUNCHED LIFEBOATS. EXPLOSION IN STEM OF SHIP. SIGHTED TORPEDO TRACK... CONTACTED LIFEBOATS 52 MEN IN WATER 2 KILLED, 1 DYING... OFF CAPE MENDOCINO." Eventually, the count would rise to five dead, one officer and four crew members, innocent victims in an unarmed ship.

A coastal lookout point was built during World War II. New lodgings were built consisting of six new dwellings built for married people, and a new large barracks for single men. After the war, the light-keepers were the only people to remain, so they moved into the new dwellings. The original lighthouse dwelling was razed along with many of the other buildings, which left only the tower standing. Without the dwelling surrounding it, the tower now required cables to help support the structure. By the end of 1948, the tower and the fog signal building were the only original structures remaining.

The station was automated in September 1953, and the fog signal station was discontinued. For the first time in 115 years, the Humboldt Bay light went unmanned. The fourth order lens was loaned to the Cabrillo National Monument for the 1955 centennial celebration. The lens was returned after the festivities, and put in service until deactivation of the Table Bluff light took place in 1972.

The tower started to fall into disrepair until in the late 1990s, when Ray Glavich donated hundreds of hours to the relocation of Table Bluff Lighthouse tower to Woodley Island. He cut it in two parts and moved it on a flat-bed truck to its destination. Glavich was also the leading force behind restoring the tower and having it reassembled into place for the public to enjoy.

HUMBOLDT HARBOUR LIGHT

In 1848, gold fever was in full swing in northern California. Tens of thousands of pioneers were heading to California from all over the world. People were heading west in wagon trains and on ships sailing for California around Cape Horn. But the west coast had not one single lighthouse. Humboldt Bay was the largest port between San Francisco and Coos Bay, Oregon. The North Spit became the Lighthouse Boards choice for Humboldt Bay's first lighthouse, one of California's original seven.

The *Oriole* supply ship was used to deliver the materials needed for the building of the lighthouses along the west coast. In 1853 the *Oriole* sunk near the mouth of the Columbia River in an infamous triangle formed by Clatsop Spit, Ledbetter Point, and Astoria, Oregon. The *Oriole's* misfortune created a delay in building the Humboldt Harbour Lighthouse.

Built by Gibbons and Kelly, the new lighthouse began operation on December 20, 1856. A 12-inch steam whistle added a first class fog-signal to the Lighthouse at North Spit in 1875. Being stationed at the Humboldt Harbour light was strenuous duty. Eureka was visible across the channel from the lighthouse but the trip was not easy. The keepers had to walk across the sand, wade out to where the station sailboat was moored, and sail across the channel. Upon their return, they would not be empty handed. Keepers would be laden with supplies to carry back across the sands of North Spit, to the lighthouse. Between its establishment in 1856, and when abandoned in 1891, 19 keepers resigned; eight were transferred, seven were "removed" (fired), three died, and one deserted.

In 1877, an earthquake cracked the foundation of the lighthouse. Another heavy quake hit in November 1878, cracking the walls of the tower and light-keepers' dwelling. The settling of the lighthouse foundation required that anchors be set in the walls every three-feet to strengthen the weakened structure. The low elevation chosen for North Spit had been a topic of criticisms for years. Having been built on the sands of the spit had increased the lighthouse's susceptibility to many natural occurrences. During its lifetime, the lighthouse endured severe earthquakes, storms, small tornados, and shifting sands. All this contributed to an exaggerated settling of the structure. Repairs were constantly required. When a storm flooded the cellar in 1885, creating even more damage, the Lighthouse Board decided to build a lighthouse on Table Bluff, and abandon Humboldt Harbour Lighthouse.

After building the Table Bluff Lighthouse, it was determined that the North Spit still required a fog signal. So in 1908, a new fog signal and keepers' dwellings were constructed near the original lighthouse location. No light was installed, instead the keepers would be in charge of maintaining three to six lanterns used to illuminate the channel entrance to

Eureka. The "Humboldt Bay Entrance Range Beacon Lights" hung from posts around the channel, guiding boaters into the heart of Eureka. For the light-keepers, the job meant precarious work. One man would maneuver the boat while the other man would grab the post, untie the cleat, retrieve the lantern, trim or replace the wick, fill the kerosene reservoir, and hoist the light back to the top of the post. They could then move on to the next light. The maneuver was tricky, and a light-keeper could wind up covered with kerosene if his timing was off. The worst light was located on the south jetty, a concrete and stone break that was subject to heavy winds and spray. The rocks were slippery with marine plants, and men often slipped and fell. The possibility of a large rogue wave was always present.

In November 1918, a severe southwestern gale caused a back up in Humboldt Bay. Both jetties were damaged and the water rose over the bulkhead, putting the spit under three to four-feet of green seawater. The fog signal building was affected and the oil house structure was undermined.

Humboldt Harbour Lighthouse
Photo courtesy of The United States Lighthouse Society

TRINIDAD HEAD LIGHTHOUSE

High atop the southwestern slope of the Trinidad headland sits Trinidad Head Lighthouse. This squat tower is only visible from a walking trail 100-yards or so above the structure. Owned and operated by the United States Coast Guard, the entire area is closed to the public.

Originally lit on December 1, 1871, the Trinidad Head Lighthouse stands a mere 25-feet tall and houses a fourth order Fresnel lens. The fog signal building, added to the property in 1898, is located 110-yards or so from the lighthouse. The deafening air horns sit next to the building waiting to alert nearby ships of heavy fog.

The most famous event in the history of this lighthouse came on December 31, 1914, when during a violent storm, light-keeper Fred L. Harrington recorded in the keepers' log:

> "The storm commenced on December 28, 1914, blowing a gale that night... I was in the tower and had just set the lens in operation and turned to wipe the lantern room windows when I observed a sea of unusual height, then about 200 yards distant, approaching. I watched it as it came in. When it struck the bluff, the jar was very heavy, and the sea shot up to the face of the bluff and over it, until the solid sea seemed to me to be on a level with where I stood in the lantern... The sea itself fell over onto the top of the bluff and struck the tower on about a level with the balcony, making a terrible jar. The whole point between the tower and the bluff was buried in water, the lens immediately stopped revolving, and the tower was shivering from the impact for several more seconds... During the 26 years I have been stationed here, there has at no time been a sea of any such size... but twice have I seen sea or spray go over pilot rock (93 feet high)."

Electricity came to Trinidad Head in 1942, after 71 years of coal oil lantern use. A modern optic replaced the lens in 1947, the same time that a new air horn took the place of the bell. The old light-keeper's dwelling

Trinidad Head Lighthouse
Photo courtesy of The United States Lighthouse Society

was torn down in 1962, and replaced with a new Coast Guard housing unit, constructed just a few feet from the tower. After automation came to the lighthouse in February 1974, the Coast Guard personnel were no longer required to live in the nearby dwellings. The beacon continues to be dutifully maintained by the United States Coast Guard.

The lighthouse is off limits to the public. Fortunately, Trinidad has a non-functioning lighthouse replica, easily accessible for tourists to visit. In 1948, Earl Hallmark donated a parcel of land, on which the Trinidad Civic Club could build an exact replica of the Trinidad Head Lighthouse. The replica was built as a memorial, paying tribute to the men from the small community who had been lost at sea. Perfectly situated, the property sits above the bay with exceptional ease of access. Located on Edwards Street at the end of Trinity Street, the memorial offers the visitor a chance to see what the real lighthouse looks like up close. The memorial displays the original fourth order Fresnel lens and 4000 pound fog bell taken from the station. These important historical artifacts give the memorial greater authenticity. For their effort, the Trinidad Civic Club received, the 1949 "Build a Better Community Contest" awarded by the National Federation of Women's Clubs.

Time and weather had taken their toll on the small tower, so in August 1998, a new stainless steel top, and new windows were installed with the help of community-minded volunteers. The real lighthouse can be seen from the headland trail which begins at the end of Edward Street. The trail leads to a viewing area about 100-yards above the station, where the lantern room can be seen.

Trinidad Head Light Station
Photo courtesy of The United States Lighthouse Society

BATTERY POINT

Battery Point Lighthouse
Photograph courtesy of the United States Lighthouse Society

On a small islet, not quite an acre in size and located just off the coast of Crescent City, sits the Battery Point Lighthouse. Surrounded by water during high tide, makes the island accessible only during low tide. A path crosses the isthmus to the island on the remains of a walkway created more than 150 years ago.

One of California's first seven lighthouses, Battery Point was built using a Cape Cod style of architecture. A single tower protrudes from the center of the small white stone building, trimmed with green. Having the light-keeper's home attached to the tower meant that during foul weather the light-keeper could tend the light without having to brave the storm. During spring, the lighthouse seems to hover in a sea of purple ice-plant, framed by Monterey cypress trees. Next to the lighthouse sits a wooden sculpture of a captain at the wheel of his ship, and a spectacular sculpture of a whale leaping from the sea. The current light-keeper's house sits adjacent to the lighthouse and is a private residence. The lighthouse, a museum and chapter of the Del Norte Historical Society, is the oldest surviving structure in Del Norte County. The main branch of the Del Norte Historical Society, located at the corner of Sixth and H Street in Crescent City, houses the great first order lens from the St. George Reef Lighthouse.

The entrance to the Crescent City Harbor was rocky and dangerous, making it evident very early on that the presence of a lighthouse was necessary. For two years, the residents placed a light on the island to help direct mariners entering the harbor.

Captain Dall, of the steamer *Columbia,* and the citizens of Crescent City made an agreement to light a lamp when the vessel was expected. Scaffolding, erected on Battery Point Island, housed a large lantern with gold reflectors.

President Franklin Pierce ordered 11 acres of land set aside for the construction of a lighthouse. The property encompassed the island, the right of way across the beach, and the property on the mainland where the parking lot and other buildings stand now. Congress appropriated the funds for the construction of a lighthouse on Battery Point in June 1856. In July, traffic to the tiny port had increased to the point where a day did not pass without a ship entering the harbor. Materials began to arrive from San Francisco in September on the barkentine *Iowana.*

Battery Point, first lit on December 10, 1856, stands 45-feet tall. Considered to be an isolated station due to the short period of time the island is accessible at low tide. Masonry, two-feet thick, acted as a mute inside the house where the sound of the surf and the fury of the storm was silenced. Battery Point was originally outfitted with a fourth order Fresnel lens, which rotated by means of a clockwork mechanism. The Clockworks were driven by a 200lb weight that dropped 26-feet down a metal tube positioned in the center of the spiral staircase that ran to the basement of the house. Every eight hours the light-keeper would rewind the mechanism.

Mr. Van Court acted as a temporary keeper until the arrival of the station's first official keeper. Theophilus Magruder arrived on Christmas Day 1856, which led to the origin of the light's local name of the "Christmas Light." Theophilus Richard Magruder migrated with his friend James Marshall from Washington DC, the home of his birth, to Oregon City. Magruder stayed for several years but in 1845, Marshall continued on to California. In 1848 Marshall would discover gold at Sutter's mill in Coloma, California, and change the course of history.

In late spring 1859, the Lighthouse Board notified light-keepers of a reduction in salary to take effect on September 1, of that year. The annual salary for Magruder had been $1,000, now reduced to $600. In September 1859, Magruder sent a letter to Washington stating that the salary reduction did not justify him staying on the job any longer past October 1, and they needed to find a replacement for him before that date.

John Heatley Jeffrey had risen through the ranks to become Captain of the 56th Massachusetts Infantry during the Civil War, serving under General Pope at the second battle of Bull Run. He married Nellie Hamilton in January 1868, and the couple left for California by way of Panama. Jeffrey entered the Lighthouse Service in 1875, in Crescent City, where he would remain for 40 years. Mrs. Jeffrey was the assistant light-keeper until October 1, 1882, when Congress once again reduced the appropriation for light-keepers' salaries and discontinued assistant light-keepers at some of the stations in the west.

During a horrific storm in 1879, Captain Jeffrey had just built a fire in the kitchen stove when a wave crashed over the island. The wave toppled over the chimney and dumped water down onto the stove, knocking it over and starting a fire. Not able to leave the safety of the lighthouse during the storm to get water, they hand pumped water from the cistern. While feverishly working to put out the fire, another wave crashed through the roof and extinguished the flames. The kitchen was a total loss.

During his tenure, Jeffrey was the target for removal from his post for his political persuasion. What follows are excerpts from three different letters: the first to Senator Barclay Henley, of the House of Representatives.

"Dear Sir: I desire to call attention to the matter of our conversation about J. H. Jeffrey, the Light House Keeper at Crescent City, Del Norte County, California. While having nothing to say concerning his competency to fill the position which he at present holds, I think it only just to the democracy of my country that he should be removed on account of active and offensive partisanship – He is a member of the Republican State Central Committee of California, a member of the Republican County Committee of Del Norte County, and has been on several occasions a delegate both to the Republican State and County Conventions. He takes an active part in local politics, and we think that justice to our party demands his removal…"

February 15, 1886 (Signed) James E. Murphy

In a letter dated February 27, 1886, Light House Inspector Philip wrote to John Jeffrey:

> "It is my desire and I shall do all in my power, to retain you in your position… The Lighthouse Board has requested me to investigate this matter and make recommendation in regard to it, in that I will visit your station this coming month to carry out its orders…"
>
> John W. Philip, Commander U.S.N.

In a letter dated March 7, 1886, John Jeffrey replied to Commander John W. Philip;

> "Sir… I have been expecting something of the kind, because Mr. Murphy, before leaving here for Washington boasted that he would get me removed on the grounds of offensive partisanship… As to the part I took in the campaign of 1884, I probably at times, when in town, have expressed a preference for Republican Candidates, never, however, at a public meeting or in what might be considered a public manor… In regard to the character of the parties mentioned. Mr. Murphy is the judge of the superior Court of the County – a politician wirepuller. A gambler & constant frequenter of liquor saloons–has the reputation of stooping to the lowest means to accomplish his ends, and generally speaking, is one of the boys and runs with that element…
>
> Thanking you for your kindness in my behalf, if I am retained in the service I shall continue to do my duty in the future as in the past."
>
> I am sir Very respectfully Your Obedient Servant
> John Jeffrey's, Keeper

In March 1914, 28 years later, John Jeffrey turned over all property to C.C. Bruehl, the new light-keeper of Battery Point. Jeffrey moved to the Point Pinos Lighthouse where he was keeper for five years. In 1915, Charles Bruehl left Battery Point and was replaced by John E. Lind. Lind had worked in the quarry that supplied the stones for St. George Reef Lighthouse and was subsequently appointed assistant light-keeper at St. George. He remained there for eight years. When he became the light-keeper of Battery Point, he and his wife Theresa moved into the beautiful little lighthouse. In 1916, light-keeper John E. Lind planted the Monterey cypress trees that inhabit the island and add such tremendous character and flair.

In 1936, electricity came to the island. A large generator, installed in the basement, could provide enough power for the residence and the beacon. The basement, known to flood sometimes during severe storms, also housed the pump used to fill the tanks above ground with water from the cistern below.

In July of 1953, Battery Point Lighthouse began a new life of automation after the Fresnel lens was retired and replaced with a 375mm dual drum lens. With no one living in the lighthouse, a small Kohler generator capable of running the beacon replaced the large generator. The following November the government officially leased the lighthouse to the Del Norte County Historical Society.

On March 27, 1964, at 5:36 p.m. Anchorage, Alaska, suffered the second largest earthquake of the twentieth century, registering 9.2 on the Richter scale. Shortly before midnight, the small coastal community of Crescent City was unaware of the earthquake that had occurred or that a massive tidal wave was traveling 500 miles an hour that would bring devastation before sunrise. Clarence Roxey Coons and his wife Etta Ella "Peggy" were the acting light-keepers of the Battery Point Lighthouse when the tsunami occurred. Peggy awoke just a little before midnight and sensed there was something amiss. She was familiar with the tides since their very existence revolved around them. This was high tide, and the sounds seemed different from usual. When she looked out at the water, she could see no rocks; even at high tide and during the most severe storms, the tops of the rocks were always visible.

Peggy hurried to wake up Roxey and tell him something was wrong. The two dressed quickly and climbed to the highest point on the island next to the flagpole. The night was clear and filled with moonlight, giving them a full view of the events about to unfold. There was an unsettling calm and stillness in the air, not even the sound of the water lapping against the shore was present. The breakwater was completely submerged, and as they stood there watching the water rise the first wave began to roll in slowly. As they looked out to sea, they saw a huge dark wall of water heading toward the city. As the wave hit the town, sounds of breaking glass and cracking wood reached the island. The two could see buildings collapse and cars being picked up and tossed around like toys. Within minutes, the wave began to recede, taking the debris of its destruction back with it into the harbor. Cars, logs, and pieces of buildings lined the beach. Boats were sitting on the land while others drifted out to sea along with a few cars and small buildings. The water receded, gathering height again about a half mile out.

A second wave rushed through town creating more damage and causing lights to go out on Front Street, but the wave did not appear as large as the first. The back flow began, and the water once again gathered outside the harbor. Then, the third wave began its way toward town; the largest wave yet, destroying everything in its path. A fire began as the water reached the south part of town. Sparks flew, when the fire ignited, filling the night sky with light. Suddenly, the water began to recede. The couple watched as the water emptied from the harbor and gathered further out to sea than it had before. The couple stood at the top of the island looking down at what no man had seen before; the bare reef, rocks, and shoals. It was "a vast labyrinth of caves, basins, and pits, undreamed of in the wildest fantasy" according to Peggy in her paper, *Crescent City's Destructive Horror of 1964*. When they rose and looked out to sea, they could see an immense wave slowly building speed as it headed for their tiny island. This massive wall of water, stretching from the barren sea floor into the night sky, appeared to the couple to be much higher than the island. When the wave hit, the water divided and whirled around both sides of the island as it passed heading for town. As it hit the shore, it tore up the debris left on the beach, picking it up and hurling it once again toward town. The pilings on the dock split and broke away from the force of the wave. When the wall of water hit Dutton's lumberyard, bundles of lumber were tossed around and broke apart. Wood split in mid air, adding to the debris as it floated through town. As the water began to recede, it seemed to suck the city back out in its wake. Everything appeared to be moving - buildings, cars, furniture, lumber, televisions, and beds all rushed past the island. The fire spread to the Texaco tanks, which began to explode one after another illuminating the night sky. The water rushed back out past the island. Each wave thereafter diminished in size, as the water seemed to slosh around the harbor settling down just around dawn. Everywhere they looked was devastation. Debris of every kind strewn in every direction, yet the island was completely spared, and the Coons did not even get their feet wet.

The waves brought widespread devastation to 56 blocks, destroying 172 businesses, 91 houses, 21 boats, and 12 house trailers. Surprisingly only 11 people were lost in the tragedy. Communications were lost. Debris covered two miles of highway 101. President Johnson declared Crescent City a disaster area. A master plan was set in place to rebuild the damage estimated between seven and 15-million dollars. The Tsunami generated by the quake also hit the Gulf of Alaska, seriously damaging Alberni, and Port Alberni, Canada.

When the U.S. General Service Administration determined that the Battery Point Lighthouse was surplus property in 1969, the government sold the property to the Del Norte County Historical Society for use as a museum. Battery Point Lighthouse was reactivated as a Private Aid to Navigation in 1982.

Battery Point Light Station
Photograph courtesy of the United States Lighthouse Society

ST. GEORGE REEF

St. George Reef Lighthouse
Photo courtesy of The United States Lighthouse Society

Following one of the worst maritime disasters on the Pacific coast, the need for a light to mark St. George Reef was certainly obvious to the Lighthouse Board and the sailors who plied the waters. It was not as obvious to Congress, who did not make the funds available for 17 years.

Located just northwest of Crescent City is St. George Reef Lighthouse, one of America's greatest lighthouse achievements. Building St. George Reef Lighthouse was a stupendous feat of engineering and also the most expensive of any lighthouse ever built. Total costs exceeded 705 thousand dollars and the project took over ten years to complete.

St. George Reef Lighthouse is a granite tower standing 90-feet tall atop Northwest Seal Rock, the last rock in a reef system that extends like a triangle from Point St. George to approximately seven miles off the coast of California. The reef is home to many rocks that show above water, and many more that are awash at low tide. Others have from three to four fathoms of water on them. They make up a dangerous reef, christened "Dragon Rocks" by English explorer George Vancouver in 1792.

On the grass-covered bluff of the mainland, is the beautiful Point St. George Wildlife Conservation Area, overlooking the majestic lighthouse. It is here that the Coast Guard station stood. Wind on the point can range from a mild breeze to a staggering wind. On a clear day, the lighthouse is visible from the bluff but for a better view, it is strongly recommended to use binoculars, or a telescope.

Once a month, between October and June, the St. George Reef Lighthouse Preservation Society sponsors helicopter flights to see this historic lighthouse, weather permitting. The six-minute flight by helicopter departs from the Cal-Ore building at the Crescent City airport, for a one-hour tour of the St. George Reef Lighthouse. Although all too brief, the helicopter ride to the lighthouse is exhilarating. Stepping out onto the caisson with the sea crashing over the rocks is truly a memorable experience. During the months between June and September, the reef is a mating sanctuary for the Northern Stellar Seal Lion and is off limits.

By 1865, the *Brother Jonathan*, a side-wheel steamer, was showing its age, she had been overused, and on a run of bad luck. Earlier that year, her engine quit on her just past the Golden Gate, and she began taking on water. The preceding trip, while on the Columbia River, the *Brother Jonathan* had collided with the sailing ship *Jane Falkenberg*, damaging the hull. Captain DeWolf reported the damage to the company and suggested hauling her out and having her repaired, but the company decided to wait and do the job at the dock.

On the morning of July 28, 1865, Samuel J. DeWolf, the tall bearded Captain of the *Brother Jonathan* was watching his ship being loaded with 700 tons of cargo. His look of despair as he watched the *Brother Jonathan* sink lower and lower into the bay gave away his overwhelming feeling of dread. DeWolf and some crew members felt the ship was dangerously overloaded. DeWolf had lodged a complaint declaring she was unsafe for the large number of passengers she was carrying. The agent told DeWolf that if he did not want to take her out he could find someone who would, so DeWolf relented. When the crew cast off, the *Brother Jonathan* had set fast into the muddy bottom of the Broadway street wharf. Tugboats towed the *Brother Jonathan* out into deep water that rose almost level with her decks. The ship arrived in Crescent City the next morning, off-loaded a small amount of cargo, and was back underway by 9:30.

During heavy weather St. George Reef "smokes" (produces thick, smoke-like spray) and the rocks can become completely obscured. Lacking seamarks, the position of the reef is almost impossible to judge.

On Thursday, April 14, 1927 the Crescent City Courier reported that in his court statement, the quartermaster from the *Brother Jonathan*, Jacob Yates said,

> "I took the wheel at twelve o'clock.
> A northwest gale was blowing, and we
> were four miles above Point St. George.
> The sea was running mountain high, and
> the ship was not making any headway.
> The Captain thought it best to turn back
> to Crescent City and wait until the storm

had ceased. He ordered the helm hard a port, I obeyed, and it steadied her. I kept due east. This was about 12:45. When we made Seal Rock, the Captain said "Southeast by south"... We ran till 1:50, when she struck with great force, knocking the passengers down and starting the deck planks... Captain DeWolf ordered everyone to look to his own safety and said that he would do the best he could for all."

The vessel, was now impaled on a jagged point on a hidden underwater ledge, which had pierced the hull. Any attempts to back her off the pinnacle were futile. The copper hull groaned as the obstruction ground violently against the bottom of the ship. The waves rocked her back and forth against the reef, ripping the vessel apart and hastening her demise. Water rushed through the gaping hole and into the aft holds. Soon after the steamer struck, the crew launched the first lifeboat, but too many people attempted to board, and it immediately capsized. Nearly all of the occupants drowned right in front of the remaining passengers; the second boat sank as well.

The third mate, James Patterson managed to lower another boat and placed five women and three children inside. Ten members of the crew jumped into the boat before Patterson could load any other passengers. These 19 people would be the only survivors of the *Brother Jonathan*. The ship went down 45 minutes after striking the rock, at least 166 persons and perhaps more than 200 drowned in what remains as California's worst shipwreck.

Among the passengers were Brigadier General George Wright and his wife. Seeing that her husband could not accompany her into the lifeboat, she refused to go ashore, choosing to stay in the arms of the man she loved. His body floated ashore, and her body was never found.

A German woman from Philadelphia, whose husband had been a newspaperman, had taken their life savings upon his death with the desire of moving to Seattle to start a small German newspaper. Before leaving the berth, she gave her son, a small boy named Paul about two years of age, a ten-cent piece to play with. After the horrific ordeal, both mother and son were among the few survivors of the shipwreck to make it ashore. Distraught, Paul was clenching his fist so tight that his little fingers had to be pried open, revealing the dime embedded in the palm of his hand.

Overloading ships was a common occurrence along the coast. In 1876, changes in the law required a Plimsoll line when loading cargo. This line, located on the side of the ship, sinks into the water as cargo is loaded, and when the line reaches the water, loading must stop, to insure safety.

The September-October 1989 issue of the *Humboldt Historian* reported that in February 1875, the 12th District Engineer wrote,

> "Northwest Seal Rock is the outermost rock of the reef. A light on this would undoubtedly be of very great benefit to general commerce, but I would conceive it a very difficult task to procure foundation for it, as the rock is exposed to the full force of the sea, with any unusual swell, the sea breaks over it."

Nevertheless, the Lighthouse Board chose Northwest Seal Rock as the location for the light. George Ballantyne, chosen as the superintendent of construction, had built the Tillamook Rock Lighthouse in Oregon under somewhat similar conditions.

A surveyor landed on the rock in October 1881, and immediately after landing the sea began to rise. It became necessary for him to leave after only one hour, but he was able to get a few rough measurements and sketches of the rock.

In April 1883, the schooner *La Ninfa* fitted for accommodation of 25 men left San Francisco in tow of the *Whitelaw*. Stored on board both ships were explosives, tools, and supplies needed for the first season's work ahead. Among the crew were quarrymen, stonecutters, and a blacksmith. After five stormy days at sea, the ships arrived at Northwest Seal Rock awash in rough seas.

Attempts to drop anchor proved futile when they found the spar buoys were too light and the water 12-fathoms deeper than anticipated. The *Whitelaw* sailed for Humboldt Bay 60 miles south to refit the spar buoys to the needed specifications. Upon its return to Northwest Seal Rock, there was no sign of the *La Ninfa* or the moorings. The weather was fine, so the remaining three moorings were set with the new heavier buoys. Ballantyne searched for five days before returning to Humboldt Bay. When the *Whitelaw* met up with the sailing ship *Josephine,* Ballantyne was informed that they had sighted the *La Ninfa* off Cape Mendocino, 25 miles southwest of Crescent City. When Ballantyne located the *La Ninfa*, he found the source of the AWOL ship. It turns out that the eight inch hawser, connecting the ship to the spar buoy, had broken, sending the buoy to follow its mooring to the bottom of the sea (two days of dragging the surrounding area never turned up the mooring). Without anchorage, the *La Ninfa* drifted south before being sighted and towed back into position. The *Whitelaw* returned and set the final mooring, and then anchored the schooner in place for the season, 300-feet from the rock.

When the first landing on the rock took place ringbolts were set, and the next day drilling began. Blasting soon started on Northwest Seal Rock to accommodate a 77,000-gallon fresh water storage tank.

Working on the construction crew for St. George Reef was a hard and dangerous life. Workers were consistently pelted with blast fragments and drenched with spray. Changing conditions sometimes required getting off the rock in a hurry. Ballantyne had a tramway built from a ring bolt set at the top of the rock; it passed between the masts of the schooner to a spar buoy moored on the outer side of the ship. Halyards hooked onto the wire picked up the slack. A cage, fashioned from planks, and a four-foot diameter iron ring transported men and supplies to and from the rock via a cable running in a continuous loop. Ballantyne was always watching the ocean. If he perceived a change in the weather or threat from the sea, he would yell a warning, and the 30 to 35 men would slash their tools to eyebolts and get to the cage. As soon as five or six men climbed aboard, Ballantyne would release the cage, and it would slide swiftly down to the schooner. A donkey engine installed on the schooner would pull on the looped cable, and the cage would return to the rock for another load. Clearing the rock with swift timing and teamwork could have the crew transported back to the *La Ninfa* in 20 minutes.

In September 1883, while drilling a deep hole, two quarrymen were washed over the rocks and down a steep slope almost 30-feet by a massive wave washing completely over the rock. They were left clinging for their lives, bruised and bleeding, until they could be rescued.

When the season's work was over the anxious crew, wanting to end their long seclusion, worked with great eagerness. On the last day of the season, tools and men were loaded on board the *La Ninfa*, and by 2 a.m. the next morning the first storm of the season had hit with such violence that every cable holding the schooner except one, had broken away. The schooner, anchored by a single line to the outer buoy rode out the raging storm for four days. The morning after the storm, the steamer *Crescent City* arrived at the rock. The *La Ninfa* cut her last remaining mooring-line and followed the steamer back in. Thus concluded the first year of construction; the rock was now ready to start receiving stones.

A contract, given to Mr. James Simpson of Eureka, to build the workers quarters on the North Spit at Humboldt Bay, was a fortuitous choice for

Ballantyne. Soon after meeting, he was informed by Simpson of a granite deposit recently found on the Mad River about five miles north of Humboldt Bay. Upon inspecting the granite, it appeared to be enough material to complete the tower. Ballantyne contacted the lighthouse engineer who secured the stone, as well as the railroad contracts to transport the stone from the quarry to the stone yard.

A great push took place at the quarry in the spring of 1884, as well as the stone yard, creating the cut stones and getting them ready for shipment to the rock. The steamer *Whitelaw,* once again proceeded to the rock to set the moorings, taking advantage of the fine early July weather. Carried onboard the *Whitelaw* was a 50-foot derrick to be placed in position and secured to the rock. The boom, 20-inches in diameter by 90-feet long, had two 78-foot long stiff support legs. From this point on there was no need to use the cage for transport to the rock. The derrick could simply pick up a boat, swing it around, and land it on the pier. At the same time, the schooner *American Boy* was chartered and fitted as a workers' quarters at the rock.

Bad news came to the whole crew when the appropriation from congress proved thoroughly inadequate for the expenditures of the season, so work on the rock ceased. The appropriation in 1885, was also inadequate, suspending work. To protect the large derrick, a work force, sent out from Humboldt Bay, secured the derrick from exposure to the heavy seas.

In four years only one season had proved productive, and of that only 100 days were utilized beneficially. Wasteful expenses, along with equipment deteriorated by exposure, rot, and rust, all combined to make the first four years of the work unduly expensive. Authority given to charter the vessels necessary and to hire laborers to start laying stone finally came in 1887.

The stonecutters in Humboldt accurately shaped each block creating a mortise and tenon joint for every stone, which would fit perfectly together. Every stone cut had to fit into a precise location. When it reached the rock it had to be an exact fit with no further work required. Each stone locked to its neighbor with hexagonal gun metal pins. The pins, two-inches in diameter, extended half its length into each stone on adjoining sides. After installation molten sulfur, poured alongside each pin, would lock them together. Each course of stones was also locked in place with large-diameter gun metal pins anchoring it to the course below.

Before the crew could go to work again, three years of neglect and inactivity on the rock needed repair. In Humboldt County at the Mad River quarry, heavy rains had turned the quarry into a mud pit, burying the railroad tracks, buildings, and many of the already quarried 1,500 stones waiting for shipment. The mast of the big derrick, previously secured on the rock, had suffered a blow from the sea some 10-feet above high water, which the men repaired with heavy iron bands. During March and April, the men worked furiously to repair damage and prepare for the work ahead.

Heavy gales were characteristic of the weather in the summer of 1887, making progress difficult and treacherous. Conditions forced the men to abandon the rock on a daily basis, but no men or materials were lost. During one such storm in June, the men had set a three and a half ton stone in place with mortar but had not yet set the dowels when they were forced to leave the rock due to bad weather. Only 12 hours later, the sea had torn the stone loose and thrown it up onto the next bench. At the close of the season, eight courses of stones were complete. Stone cutting at Humboldt Bay proceeded during the winter, but suspended in March due to of lack of funds.

When the steamer schooner *Del Norte* arrived for the 1888 season in May, the wharf was finished and moorings reset. Quarters to accommodate 50 men were built next to the pier, derricks were erected, and the hoisting engine was set in place. By the end of the season, 13 courses of masonry now brought the height of the pier to 28-feet. The pier was anchored into "zero course" (a four-foot thick concrete base set into the rock). The workers could now live in quarters constructed on the rock. This meant they could lay masonry as fast as the stones could reach them. Work began on the 14th course of stones at the end of April 1889. The quarters built on the rock the previous year were badly damaged in the eight-month hiatus from the rock and required repair. Later in the season a huge gale smashed them again at 2:00 a.m.. No one was hurt, but some of the men were washed out of their bunks. By the beginning of October, more courses of stone had been set. The walls of the boiler room, coal room, and storage rooms were complete at season's end.

In July 1890, all the stones required for completion of the station were secured. The stone yard and the Humboldt quarry closed, and the men were discharged. Funds were not available for summer 1890, leaving the rock abandoned for another year.

Upon arrival in April 1891, the workers found the quarters destroyed by the sea, having to rebuild them once again. The mooring buoys had disappeared, but two of the buoys were found and reset; the remaining two buoys were replaced. Construction, back on track by May, had the quarters repaired, the derricks set, and weather permitting everyone pushed toward completion. Although April and May had considerable rain and heavy seas, the rest of the season held favorable weather. The first stone was set on May 13, the last on August 23, leaving more than two months to remove the scaffolding, erect ironwork, put concrete arches in the tower, and pour concrete floors. A myriad of other finishing tasks took place, including painting, plastering, varnishing, and the setting up of all of the machinery. Construction was complete by the end of October with the exception of the lens, but the men could not get off the rock for another week and a half due to heavy seas. Finally, the moorings were lifted. The men loaded the rigging and tools onto the ship and left the station in the hands of three keepers, who watched the ship as it sailed off for San Francisco.

The surface of the station's pier acted as a watershed, covered with 12 inch thick flagging stone from the center of the pier to the outer edge. A three-inch fall allowed water to run off into gutters cut in the stone. The water then ran down pipes that led to the cistern located in the base of the pier. To prevent leakage, a mixture of sand and cement, slightly moistened with boiled linseed oil was used as caulking between the joints.

The light-keepers' rooms were all adorned with tongue and groove hardwood floors of seasoned Humboldt pine. Wainscoting of Port Orford cedar with redwood panels lined the walls, oak doors and windows were all varnished and polished to a shine.

At completion, 1,339 dressed stones made up the pier, none weighing less than two tons and many weighing six. In total there are 14,000 tons of stone in the entire structure. The first order Fresnel lens reached San Francisco in July 1892, and was constructed within the lantern room in August, where it was exhibited for the first time on October 20, 1892. The fog signal at Saint George Reef that began as a steam-powered 12-inch whistle, changed to an air siren in 1931, and then to an air powered diaphone horn in 1936.

In the ten years that it took to assemble the lighthouse, surprisingly, only one life was lost. In fact, this was the only serious injury to take place during construction. In June 1891, after letting go of a tag line, a rigger was carried over the pier and killed.

Duty on the "Dragon" was a dangerous assignment. Within the first year of operation, assistant keeper William Ericcson, after setting out for Crescent City in a standard station boat, never made it to his destination. He and the boat were never found.

Storms could rage for days, leaving keepers stranded for extended periods. Keepers were on a rotation of two weeks on and two weeks off, weather permitting. If the weather did not cooperate the schedule could easily change. The station was out of communication for 59 days in 1937. The weather was so bad that no tender could even get close enough to deliver the mail or to leave the desperately needed food and supplies for the crew. The four men on duty did not speak to each other for almost a month. In February of 1974, the Coast Guard News Public Affairs Office distributed a press release where Light-keeper George Roux was quoted as saying;

> "After the first four weeks, we were
> so talked out and thought out that just to
> say 'Please pass the salt' or 'Lousy day
> today, ain't it?' Became a serious personal
> affront. It got so bad that we would try
> to ignore the presence of each other to
> avoid scraps. This despite our being
> solid friends for years. Funny thing, the
> moment the weather pressure let up and
> life in the tower returned to normal, so did
> our pressures and we returned to normal,
> too. We were friends again, talked our
> heads off."

George Permenter was the officer in-charge of the light on April 5, 1951, when the worst accident in California lighthouse history occurred. After swinging the station boat out over the water with five coastguardsmen aboard, Permenter gauged the waves and dropped the boat into the trough between two waves. Everything went like clockwork, but as he watched the crew release the bridle, a huge wave picked up the launch and tossed it toward the rock. The backwash of the wave from the rock inundated the boat throwing the five men into the frigid water. Permenter jumped from 20-feet into the sea and rescued two of the men clinging to the mooring buoy. He was unable to save the other three coastguardsmen. Stanley Costello, Bertram C. Beckett Jr., and Wilber J. Walker died in the tragedy. George Permenter was awarded the Silver Life-Saving Medal for his efforts.

The lighthouse was decommissioned on May 13, 1975, and the huge iron doors closed for the last time. The colors were lowered, and St. George Reef Lighthouse was left to the ocean and the elements. The beacon was replaced with a large navigation buoy that measured 400-feet in diameter. The buoy, outfitted with a light, radio beacon, and foghorn and was located a mile from the lighthouse.

The lighthouse lay abandoned until August 1983, when Bob Bolen, Wayne Wheeler, and Diana Miller arrived on the Coast Guard Cutter *Blackhaw* in preparation to dismantle the first order lens from the St. George Reef Lighthouse, and transport it to the Del Norte Historical

Society's main museum downtown.

The first order Fresnel lens was carefully lowered from the tower to the deck of the lighthouse one piece at a time, using a 10-foot boom. Anchored about 250-feet away, the *Blackhaw* had a line running to the lighthouse. Each lens piece was sandwiched between old surplus mattresses and pulled along the line to the boat. At Crescent City, the pieces, placed on a flatbed truck, were transported to the museum. Bob Bolen and Dave George reassembled the lens from 36 crates in all, each weighing about 250 pounds. The job took four months to complete, aided by the original numbers placed on by the maker. The assembled lens stands 18.5-feet high, seven-feet wide, and weighs more than two tons. Bob Bolen donated the annex to the Del Norte Historical Society. The annex was designed to hold the beautifully restored first order Fresnel lens from St. George Reef Lighthouse.

The Del Norte Historical Society is also the home to many artifacts from the ill fated *Brother Jonathan.* Discovered in February 1994, the *Brother Jonathan* ultimately yielded 1,207 gold coins. The Supreme Court of the United States heard the case of California verses Deep Sea Research, (who salvaged the ship). The decision mandated 20 percent would go to the State of California. In 1999, the remaining treasure went up for auction.

Designated as a National monument, St. George Reef Lighthouse is now privately operated by the "St. George Reef Light Preservation Society."

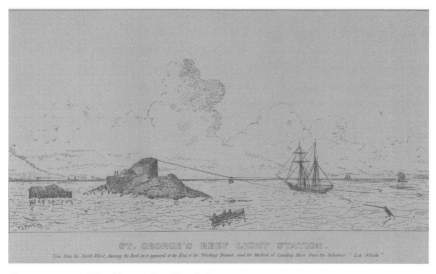

Construction of St. George Reef Lighthouse
Photo courtesy of The United States Lighthouse Society

BIBLIOGRAPHY

Most information was derived from; Annual Reports of the Lighthouse
Board and Lighthouse Service, diaries and personal letters.
Charles S. Greene, *Los Farallones De Los Fraylas*
(Overland Monthly, September 1892)
Charles Nordhoff, *The Farallon Islands*
(Harpers New Monthly, April 1874)
Mildred Brooke Hoover, *The Farallon Islands*
(Stanford University Press, April 5 1932)
Early West Coast Lighthouses
(San Francisco: Book Club of California, 1964)
Robin W. Doughty, *San Francisco's Nineteenth Century Egg Basket*
(The Geographical Review, October 1969)
Joseph E. Brown, *Cabrillo National Monument*
(Cabrillo Historical Association 1981)
John Soennichsen, *Miwoks to Missiles*
(Angel Island Association 2001)
Frederick Stonehouse, *Lighthouse Keepers and Coast Guard Cutters*
(Gwinn, Michigan Avery Color Studios 2000)
Norma Engle, *Three Beams of Light*
(San Diego: Tecolote Publications 1986)
Ralph Shanks and Lisa Woo Shanks, *Guardians Of The Golden Gate*
(Petaluma: Costano Books 1975)
Ralph Shanks and Janetta Thompson Shanks,
Lighthouses and Lifeboats on the Redwood Coast
(Petaluma: Costano Books 1978)
Sharlene & Ted Nelson, *Umbrella Guide to California Lighthouses*
(Kenmore: Epicenter Press Inc. 1993)
Geneva Hamilton, *Where the Highway Ends: A history of Cambria*
(San Luis Obispo: Central Coast Press 1974)
Mary Louise Clifford / J. Candace Clifford, *Women Who Kept the Lights*
(Alexandria: Cypress Communications 2000)
Battery Point and St. George Reef Lighthouses
(Medford, Oregon: Webb Research Group Publishers 2000)
John A. Martini, *Fort Point: Sentry at the Golden Gate*
(San Francisco: Golden Gate National Park Association 1991)
Bion B. Williams, *The Santa Barbara Light, and its Keeper*

Frank Perry, *East Brother; History of a Light Station*

Colleen MacNeney, *New England Lighthouse Thought To Have Been Destroyed Found In California* (Lighthouse Digest 2008)

Index

A

A.C. Freese 95
Active 68, 128
Aculeo 77
Agwiworld 65
Alcatraz 3, 6, 7, 14, 102, 109, 122, 162
American Boy 189
Anacapa 3, 14, 38, 41, 43
Anacapa Island 14, 38, 41, 43
Angel Island 2, 3, 64, 99, 101, 109, 114, 151
Angels Gate 14, 26, 30, 36
Año Nuevo 70, 72, 114
Arvel Settles 52

B

Battery Point 177, 183
Bibliography 194
B. M. Watson 88
Ballantyne 187, 188
Ballast Point 14, 19, 20, 21, 22, 24, 170
Barbier & Benard 40
Battery Point 3, 7, 14, 19, 61, 111, 158, 177, 181, 183
Bear 164
Bishop 143
Blackhaw 192
Blunts Reef 163, 164
Bob Bolen 192
Brother Jonathan 185, 193
Bureau of Land Management 57, 161

C

Cabrillo National Monument 2, 19, 21, 23, 171
Cambria 56
Cape Mendocino 3, 14, 88, 114, 140, 148, 152, 161, 163, 164, 166, 167, 168, 169, 171, 187
Carquinez 1, 3, 14, 86, 87, 88, 89

Carrier Pigeon 74
Channel Islands National Park 41, 43
Charles F. Allen 40
Charles J. McDougal 88
Charles Layton 61
Charlotte Layton 44
Coast Guard 1, 3, 8, 23, 30, 35, 37, 40, 42, 52, 57, 60, 65, 69, 72, 74, 84, 85, 90, 96, 97, 102, 110, 121, 124, 134, 145, 151, 152, 155, 156, 159, 160, 163, 165, 169, 174, 175, 184, 192
Colombian Exposition 23
Columbia 7, 76, 128, 162, 172, 178, 185
Corwin 143
Crescent City 14, 19, 177, 179, 181, 183, 184, 185, 187, 188, 191, 193

D

Dave George 193
Del Norte 2, 177, 179, 181, 183, 190, 193
Del Norte Historical Society 2, 177, 193
Delpha Atkinson 133
Destroyer Squadron Eleven 50, 51
Diana Miller 192

E

E.A. Bryan 83, 84
Earthquake 113, 157
East Brother 1, 3, 6, 14, 88, 93, 95, 97, 99, 112
Edward H. Watson 50
Emidio 152, 171
Emily Fish 64, 65
Hermann and Freda Engle 91
Eureka 124, 170, 172, 173, 188

F

Farallon 7, 11, 75, 125, 126, 127, 128,

129, 130, 132, 135, 153
Farallon Egg Company 126, 129
Farallone O'Caine 133
Fort Guijarros 20
Fort Point 3, 7, 14, 61, 102, 111, 112, 113, 117, 118, 122
Fred Kreth 145
Fredrick Little Jordan 117
Augustin Fresnel 11

G

Gaynel Dresser 120
George Ballantyne 187
George Fake 58
George Hooke 148
George Parkinson 46
George Permenter 192
George Putnam 7
George Shaw 32
George Vancouver 31, 184
Gibbons & Kelly 7
Glen Cove Marina 87
Golden Gate Bridge 109, 111, 113, 114, 115, 116, 117, 122
Gotford Olson 52
Grace Dollar 164

H

Hartman Bache 46, 128
Hearst Castle 57
Adna E. Hecox 67
Henderson 50, 59, 64
Henri Le Paute 22
Henry Bergh 134
Henry E. Nichols 64
Henry Randall 47, 48
Honda Point 50
USS Chauncey 52
USS Delphy 50
USS Farragut 51
USS Fuller 51
USS Percival 51
USS S.P. Lee 51
USS Young 51

Humboldt Harbour 7, 40, 114, 172

I

India Bear 116
Iowana 178

J

J.C. Ryan 72
James A. McMahon 119
James Rankin 112
James W. Marshall 6, 178
Jane Falkenberg 185
Jesse Mygrants 52
John Drake Sloat 19
John E. Lind 181
John Emory Thorndyke 56
John Heatley Jeffrey 179
Albert Joost 99, 100
Jose Mario Arguello 50
Josephine 187
Juan Cabrillo 19
Julia F. Williams 45

K

Kate C. McDougal 89
Kennedy 52

L

La Ninfa 187, 188
Laura Hecox 67, 68
Leader 95
Library of Congress 31
Liebre 42
Lighthouse Board 7, 14, 19, 21, 22, 31, 41, 46, 49, 56, 64, 68, 86, 89, 93, 111, 112, 122, 123, 125, 129, 130, 132, 140, 143, 148, 162, 168, 170, 172, 178, 180, 184
Lighthouse Bureau 8
Lighthouse Service 7, 11, 23, 32, 37, 40, 79, 102, 112, 117, 126, 130, 132, 134, 145, 148, 151, 163,

179
Lightship WLV-605 163
Lime Point 114, 115, 116, 117, 148
Long Beach Robot Light 4, 26
Lorin Vincent Thorndyke 56
Louise Johnson 133
Lucas 128
Luce, Allen L. 63

M

Madrono 131, 132
Mal Combs Park 166
Manzanita 88, 130, 168
Mare Island 14, 88, 89, 102, 168
Mark Abbott Memorial Lighthouse 66
Mary L. Smith 32
Mercury 11, 150, 155
Mile Rock 14, 117, 118, 119, 120, 121
Monterey 19, 44, 58, 60, 61, 62, 64, 65, 67, 68, 114, 177, 181

N

Newark 91
New Point Loma 14, 19, 21, 22, 23
Nicholas 51
North Seal Rock 133
North Spit 40, 170, 171, 172, 189
Novick 140

O

Oakland Harbor 3, 14, 66, 90, 91
Old Point Loma 3, 14, 19, 20, 21, 22, 23
Oriole 7, 61, 126, 172
Oscar Johnson 34
Bill Owens 150, 152, 159
Cora Isabel Owens 154, 159

P

Pacific Enterprise 153, 154
Pacific Grove 14, 61, 63, 65
Paul Hamilton 52
Paul J. Pelz 31
Piedras Blancas 57
Pigeon Point 65, 71, 72, 74, 75, 76,

77, 146
Pinedorado Grounds 57
Point Arena 1, 3, 14, 33, 74, 147, 149, 150, 152, 153, 159
Point Arguello 14, 46, 50, 51, 64, 132
Point Blunt 108
Point Bonita 3, 6, 14, 115, 117, 122, 123, 124, 140
Point Buchon 56
Point Cabrillo 1, 3, 14, 50, 93, 150, 156, 157, 158, 159
Point Conception 7, 11, 14, 33, 36, 45, 46, 47, 48, 49, 55, 102, 151, 159, 161
Point Delgado 166
Point Diablo 115, 117, 119
Point Fermin 1, 3, 14, 32, 33, 34, 36, 39
Point Hueneme 14, 36, 40, 41, 50
Point Knox 64, 109, 114
Point Lobos 120
Point Loma 3, 7, 14, 19, 20, 21, 22, 24, 36, 121
Point Montara 1, 3, 14, 74, 77, 83, 114
Point Pedernales 50
Point Pinos 3, 7, 14, 19, 44, 55, 61, 64, 65, 69, 111, 148, 181
Point Reyes 6, 3, 14, 125, 132, 139, 142, 143, 145, 167
Point Stuart 109
Point Sur 3, 58, 60, 65, 114, 151, 159
Point Vicente 1, 14, 36, 37, 45
Port Chicago 14, 83
Port Hueneme 14, 32, 40
Punta Gorda 3, 14, 162, 167

Q

Quinault Victory 83, 84, 85

R

Ray Glavich 171
Relief 164, 165
Richard Bard 40
Rio de Janeiro 112, 117, 119
Robert Hubert 86

Robert Louis Stevenson 63
Robot Light 26
Roe Island 14, 83, 84, 85
Rubicon Point 79

S

Sandy Tucker 76
San Luis Obispo 2, 3, 14, 24, 56
San Pablo Bay 86, 88, 93, 112
Santa Barbara 1, 14, 38, 39, 41, 44,
    45, 46, 50, 65, 68
Santa Cruz 4, 14, 38, 66, 67, 69, 72,
    75, 92
Santa Rosa 50
Sea Nymph 140
Sebastian Vizcaino 24, 58, 61, 70
Shelter Cove 169
Shubrick 128, 167
Simon F. Blunt 38
Sir Francis Drake 125
Solar power 8, 43
Somers 51
Sonora 47
Southampton Shoals 1, 3, 14, 100,
    101
St. Francis Yacht Club 1, 101
St. George Reef 1, 3, 14, 133, 170,
    177, 181, 184, 185, 187, 188,
    189, 191, 193, 194, 200
St. Joseph 127
State Parks 58, 74, 76, 79, 160
Stoddert 52
Suisun Bay 83, 86

T

Table Bluff 3, 14, 21, 40, 170
Tennessee 122
Thelma Austin 33
Theophilus Richard Magruder 178
Theresa C. Watson 88
Thomas Atkinson 133
Thompson 52
Trinidad 174, 175

U

United States Coast Guard, USCG
    110, 124, 174, 175
United States Lighthouse Society 1,
    193
USS California 42
USS Chicago 132
USS Macon 59

V

Vallejo 2, 86, 88
Ventura 2, 41, 58
Vizcaino 24, 58, 61, 70
Alexander Volta 132

W

Walter White 148, 150
Walton Light 66
Warrior Queen 142
Wayne Wheeler 192
Whitelaw 187, 189
Willard Miller 95, 96
William Lewis Austin 33
William Mollering 59
Albert J. Williams 44
William Ward 117
Winfield Scott 38, 39, 41
Woodbury 51, 52

Y

Yankee Blade 47, 48
Yerba Buena 6, 8, 14, 49, 91, 100,
    102, 109, 112

RECOMMENDED WEBSITES

THE UNITED STATES LIGHTHOUSE SOCIETY

WWW.USLHS.ORG

OFFICIAL LIGHTHOUSE SITES

Alcatraz http://www.nps.gov/alca/
Anacapa
http://www.nps.gov/chis/planyourvisit/island-facts-anacapa-island.htm
Angel Island http://www.angelisland.org/
Año Nuevo http://www.parks.ca.gov/default.asp?page_id=22264
Battery Point http://www.delnortehistory.org/lighthouse/
East Brother Light Station http://www.ebls.org/
Fort Point http://www.nps.gov/archive/fopo/exhibits/lighthouse/lite.htm
Oakland / Quinn's Lighthouse http://www.quinnslighthouse.com/
Parkers http://www.selectrestaurants.com/parkerslight/
Piedras Blancas
http://www.blm.gov/ca/st/en/fo/bakersfield/Programs/pbls.html
Pigeon Point http://www.parks.ca.gov/?page_id=533
Point Arena http://www.mcn.org/1/palight/
Point Cabrillo http://www.pointcabrillo.org/
Point Fermin http://www.sanpedrochamber.com/champint/ptfmlths.htm
Point Loma http://www.nps.gov/archive/cabr/lighthouse.html
Point Montara http://norcalhostels.org/montara/
Point Pinos http://www.pgmuseum.org/Lighthouse.htm
Point Reyes http://www.nps.gov/pore/history_maritime_lgthse.htm
Point Sur http://www.parks.ca.gov/default.asp?page_id=565
San Luis Obispo http://www.sanluislighthouse.org/html/index.html
St. George Reef http://www.stgeorgereeflighthouse.us/